BOX CLEVER

QUADRANTS TO CHANGE THE WAY WE LIVE AND LEAD

RACHEL JOHNSON

Together we unlock every learner's unique potential

At Hachette Learning (formerly Hodder Education), there's one thing we're certain about. No two students learn the same way. That's why our approach to teaching begins by recognising the needs of individuals first.

Our mission is to allow every learner to fulfil their unique potential by empowering those who teach them. From our expert teaching and learning resources to our digital educational tools that make learning easier and more accessible for all, we provide solutions designed to maximise the impact of learning for every teacher, parent and student.

Aligned to our parent company, Hachette Livre, founded in 1826, we pride ourselves on being a learning solutions provider with a global footprint.

www.hachettelearning.com

Although every effort has been made to ensure that website addresses are correct at time of going to press, Hachette Learning cannot be held responsible for the content of any website mentioned in this book. It is sometimes possible to find a relocated web page by typing in the address of the home page for a website in the URL window of your browser.

Hachette UK's policy is to use papers that are natural, renewable and recyclable products and made from wood grown in well-managed forests and other controlled sources. The logging and manufacturing processes are expected to conform to the environmental regulations of the country of origin.

To order, please visit www.HachetteLearning.com or contact Customer Service at education@hachette.co.uk / +44 (0)1235 827827.

ISBN: 978 1 0360 0730 0

© Rachel Johnson 2025

First published in 2025 by
Hachette Learning,
An Hachette UK Company
Carmelite House
50 Victoria Embankment
London EC4Y 0DZ
www.HachetteLearning.com

The authorised representative in the EEA is Hachette Ireland, 8 Castlecourt Centre, Dublin 15, D15 XTP3, Ireland (email: info@hbgi.ie)

Impression number   10 9 8 7 6 5 4 3 2 1
Year   2029 2028 2027 2026 2025

All rights reserved. Apart from any use permitted under UK copyright law, no part of this publication may be reproduced or transmitted in any form or by any means, electronic or mechanical, including photocopying and recording, or held within any information storage and retrieval system, without permission in writing from the publisher or under licence from the Copyright Licensing Agency Limited. Further details of such licences (for reprographic reproduction) may be obtained from the Copyright Licensing Agency Limited, www.cla.co.uk

Illustrations by DC Graphic Design Limited, Hextable, Kent
Typeset in the UK.
Printed in the UK.

A catalogue record for this title is available from the British Library.

PRAISE FOR *BOX CLEVER*

This book has allowed me to have a look at myself from the inside – how I live my life, the people I surround myself with as well as a fresh perspective on my leadership. I have critiqued myself, patted myself on the back, challenged myself but above all been gripped. Each quadrant has a purpose and turns what we do everyday upside down! This book will become a source of easy reference for future.

Carol Blackford-Mills
Managing director, MRS Digital

If you're looking to enhance your leadership skills and take your decision-making to the next level, Rachel's new book is a must-read. Each of the 11 quadrants help simplify complex challenges into actionable strategies, making it easier to manage conflict, prioritise tasks, and focus on what really matters. Like eating a boiled sweet I would recommend taking your time and working through the suggested exercises to make sure you turn each key insight into leadership tools to help you and those you work with to achieve measurable success. Quite simply this is a fantastic resource for any leader eager to grow and navigate their responsibilities with confidence!

Ken Matthews
Senior minister, St Joseph's Church, Benwell

Box Clever is a trusted guide that systematically explains complex topics in an incredibly simple way which is what we all need right now. It feels as though you are personally being walked through each step holding up a mirror to your own leadership whilst cleverly meeting you where you are at. It is challenging and at times uncomfortable but then gives practical examples and prompt questions to help you move forward. It is a clear call to action to be brave in your leadership and your reflection, for yourself and those in your team.

It is a quick read that I will keep in my work bag to give me options in team meetings, when self-reflecting, when feeling stuck or ready to try something new. I can see so many of my own experiences play out in the examples Rachel gives which is both reassuring and energising.

Danielle Haxby
Director of Education, The Green Room Foundation

Box Clever both engages and simplifies how we think about leadership through eleven existing quadrant frameworks. Rachel Johnson masterfully breaks down complex leadership challenges into clear, actionable insights that will support you along your leadership journey. Whether you're an experienced leader or just starting out, Johnson's unique approach combines self-reflection with practical strategies for growth and improvement. Each quadrant serves as both a mirror and a roadmap, helping leaders understand where they are and chart a course for where they want to be. This guide will spark essential conversations about leadership at every level, from personal development to organisational change, with a beautiful blend of accessibility and depth. *Box Clever* isn't just a book about leadership — it's a tool for reimagining meaningful impact.

Erik Ellefsen
Director of Networks and Improvement,
Baylor Center for School Leadership, Texas, USA

Box Clever proves that a few simple lines on a page can shift how you think and help you sort your life out. Rachel's no-nonsense wisdom, combined with her genius pledge cards, makes this the kind of book you'll read, use and then force on everyone you know!

Laura McInerney
Co-Founder of Teacher Tapp & Education Intelligence

Box Clever is unwaveringly practical. There's no grandstanding or jargon here, only straightforward, actionable advice. Rachel doesn't just tell you that self-reflection is important; she hands you a quadrant to map it out and determine exactly where you stand. It's like having a switched-on mentor in book form.

If you want a leadership book that gives you practical tools to structure your thinking and make decisions with confidence, *Box Clever* could be just what you've been looking for.

Steve Moss
Executive Coach and Board Member

ABOUT THE AUTHOR

Rachel Johnson is an author, leadership coach, podcaster and leadership thinker who is also the CEO of PiXL, a school leadership networking organisation working with thousands of schools across the UK and overseas. She is the host of two popular podcasts: the bite sized leadership reflections in PiXL Pearls; and the PiXL Leadership Bookclub, where two school leaders discuss a non-educational leadership book and the lessons they have learned and implemented as a result. Rachel also leads the School of PiXL Leadership, a series of courses delivered to over 2000 people each year. *Box Clever* is Rachel's third book.

To Paul, who is there consistently, lovingly and patiently, whatever life throws our way.

CONTENTS

Praise for *Box Clever* iii
About the author v
Introduction ix
Chapter 1   The one about self-reflection 1
Chapter 2   The one about conflict 11
Chapter 3   The one about self-belief and challenge 19
Chapter 4   The one about brutal facts and hope 29
Chapter 5   The one about fulfilment and boundaries 39
Chapter 6   The one about identity 49
Chapter 7   The one about timing 57
Chapter 8   The one about paradoxical thinking 63
Chapter 9   The one about issues over time 75
Chapter 10 The one about our energy 85
Chapter 11 The one about what we spend our time on 93
Final thoughts 99
Appendix 1 – Recommended resources 103
Appendix 2 – Copies of all the quadrants 107
Bibliography 119
Acknowledgements 123

INTRODUCTION

For a number of years now, I have been obsessed with quadrants – I realise that this is a niche area! This book is made up of the 'greatest hits' of quadrants that I have found helpful in my own life and leadership. I hope that after reading *Box Clever*, you may join the quadrant fan club!

Quadrants are a paradox; they are both incredibly complex and liberatingly simple. They are made up of two different concepts, placed against each other to unearth four positions that can be seen and understood at first glance. Each box is named, and the more you look at the differing positions the more you understand. They are a brilliant way of making quite intangible things tangible.

From a very young age I have been fascinated with how we make the abstract more concrete. I remember as a 13-year-old asking my teachers what we were going to do about bullying or crime or litter. We had listened to the assemblies about all three being an issue, but where was the call to action? What exactly was I meant to do? Although I have always loved listening to people talk or write about the big ideas, if I don't leave with things to implement or change I get frustrated. It's all very well talking big concepts and ideas, but my mind always goes to questions like:

- What does this mean for me or my team?
- How do I do that?
- What do I do now?
- Where am I and where do I want to be?
- How am I going to get there?
- What do I need to change?

I want to go down the rabbit holes of research and evidence, but first I need a way in. A portal that makes things simple, a way of diagnosing quickly where I think I am and where I want to be. For me, quadrants are that portal into a world of understanding and nuance.

The quadrants you are about to dive into have been collected or created over several years, and I hope they will help you identify where you are and where you want to be. This changes as we change, and our contexts change. There isn't one place in the quadrant we have to be for the rest of our lives – firstly, it would be impossible, and secondly, it wouldn't be helpful. A large part of leadership is working out where we need to be for *this* moment and why. Understanding *why* we are where we are and asking ourselves, 'Is this where I need to be right now?' is what makes our leadership deliberate and not accidental.

The book you're holding is called *Box Clever*. The definition of this term is: 'To be very careful and clever in the way that you behave in a difficult situation, so that you can get an advantage over other people'. I have no problem with the first half of this definition, but what about the second half? This book isn't about getting advantage *over* – it is about giving advantage *to* ourselves and others. It is about how we can be leaders who can give people an advantage and remove some of the things that are limiting both us and them. It is about what we need to dial up and what we need to dial down based on where we find ourselves. It is a collection of quadrants that may help you see more clearly so you can lead more clearly.

If we can 'box clever', we can use these quadrants to shed new light on familiar problems, and they can help us move to a different place. There will be plenty of difficult situations in our lives and in our leadership; my hope is that this book will help you unlock what those problems may be, find a language to express them, and help you do something about it so that we and the people we lead benefit.

You will find some of the quadrants easier than others, some more relevant than others, and you may agree with some and disagree with others. This is the point. Thinking happens when we engage with the quadrants, when we have debates in our own heads and when we explore something we may find challenging.

How to use this book

How you use this book is entirely up to you, but here are some practical suggestions that you may want to consider:

1. Start at the beginning and work through it, answering the questions and having discussions with yourself.

2. Use it like a prescription – identify the issue you want to explore and dive straight into it. Each quadrant is called 'The one about…' so you can navigate to the right place!
3. Use it as a discussion tool with your team and identify which areas are the ones you want to work on the most as a group. Use it as a basis for discussion.
4. Use it as a reflection tool to help you change over time. Write the date in the box that best describes you at that time, work on making the change and then come back to see where you are in a few weeks or months. Use it to chart your own change and then celebrate it.
5. Use the quadrants as an easy way in and then dive into all the recommended reading at the end of the book to go down your own rabbit holes.
6. Look at the quadrants and discuss them – what do you like and what do you not like about the label or the concept? What would you do instead?

A health warning!

As you read this book, I want you to remember the following things:

- You are a wonderfully complex and nuanced human being.
- No box will ever be able to define all that you are and could be.
- You are capable of change.
- These quadrants may reflect attitudes you have or positions you find yourself in, but they are not a fixed place, and they are not your identity.
- You are capable of more than you think.
- Change begins with grappling with issues.
- Don't box yourself in. Be kind to yourself – use the words 'I notice that I' rather than 'I am'.

Now you're ready to dive straight into 11 little boxes that can help you in your life and in your leadership, so you know where you need to put your weight and attention. When you know that, you can be more deliberate about your choices and your behaviour. That is when change happens.

CHAPTER 1
THE ONE ABOUT SELF-REFLECTION

Starting this book with a quadrant about our own self-perception seems a good place to start! One of the most famous quadrants when it comes to how well we know ourselves is Johari's Window. Although you have probably heard of this quadrant before, you may not have done anything more than reference it in passing. Used as it was originally intended, this quadrant is a powerful tool to help us identify where we need to focus.

	Known to self	Not known to self
Known to others	Open area	Blind spot
Not known to others	Hidden area	Unknown

Devised by psychologists Joseph Luft and Harry Ingham in 1955, Johari's Window (named after combining their two forenames) is used the world over to help people see how they perceive themselves and how other people perceive them. Through their work, Luft and Ingham realised there was a gap between these two perspectives and that there are some things we just don't know about ourselves that others do know about us. Thus, Johari's Window was born.

Johari's Window is a self-awareness tool designed to improve our interpersonal communication while also helping our personal development. The way it worked originally – although it has been widely adapted since – was that a person would be given a list of 55 characteristics and would select 5–10 that they felt represented their personality. Their colleagues or friends would then be given the same list of 55 and also be asked to select 5–10 that they felt were relevant to them. A comparison would then be made between what the person thinks and recognises about themselves and what others have said about them.

The window has since morphed into a tool that can also be used in different ways too. Donald Rumsfeld (2002) used it to talk about political situations during a press briefing:

> Reports that say something hasn't happened are always interesting to me because as we know, there are known knowns: there are things we know we know. We also know there are known unknowns: that is to say, we know there are some things [we know] we do not know. But there are also unknown unknowns: the ones we don't know we don't know. And if one looks throughout the history of our country and other free countries, it is the latter category that tends to be the difficult one.

How self-aware we are can really impact on other people. Johari's Window can help us know ourselves more and see if what we think about ourselves is the same as what others think. It can be helpful in the following ways:

- Self-awareness can link with happiness. At the very top of Maslow's hierarchy of needs is 'self-actualisation', which Maslow believed was linked to happiness. When we have an accurate view of ourselves it can build confidence and belief, which can lead to happiness.
- Using this tool, we can see where we may be overestimating our competence or characteristics, which is known as the Dunning-Kruger effect. It is better to know the reality of our abilities!
- It can help us see our strengths in a different way and what those strengths mean to other people.
- We can find a new appreciation for the characteristics that we may not recognise about ourselves.
- It is an easy way to get feedback from colleagues because it is specific and can be anonymous.
- It can work with individuals and teams and can also be amended so it is used to ascertain what you know about a situation at work.

Unpacking the boxes: Where am I now?

The purpose of Johari's Window is to find out how self-aware you are by completing your own version. At the end of the exercise, you will end up with a list of words in each box, and where they are placed shows you what you know and what you may not know about yourself.

The four different boxes are:

1. The open box – known to others, known to self.
2. The hidden box – not known to others, known to self.
3. The unknown box – not known to others, not known to self.
4. The blind-spot box – not known to self, known to others.

Here's how you can create your own Johari's Window in seven easy steps.

Step 1

From the adjectives below, choose 5–10 that you feel best describe you, write them on a piece of paper and keep them until step 3 is done. These are the things you know about yourself.

Able	Dependable	Intelligent	Patient	Sensible
Accepting	Dignified	Introverted	Powerful	Sentimental
Adaptable	Energetic	Kind	Proud	Shy
Bold	Extroverted	Knowledgeable	Quiet	Silly
Brave	Friendly	Logical	Reflective	Spontaneous
Calm	Giving	Loving	Relaxed	Sympathetic
Caring	Happy	Mature	Religious	Tense
Cheerful	Helpful	Modest	Responsive	Trustworthy
Clever	Idealistic	Nervous	Searching	Warm
Complex	Independent	Observant	Self-assertive	Wise
Confident	Ingenious	Organised	Self-conscious	Witty

Step 2

Now choose some colleagues or friends, perhaps from different areas of your life, provide them with the adjectives and ask them to choose 5–10 they believe best describe you.

Step 3

Look at what your colleagues or friends have selected alongside your list and look for the adjectives that match, then write the words that appear on both your and their list into the 'open' box. These are the characteristics that you see about yourself and other people see too; they are openly seen and acknowledged both by you and them. The more words in this area that have been chosen by you and others, the better the group dynamics may be because you share the same understanding. Expanding this area – which benefits everyone – requires communication and openness with your colleagues. Any leftover words that you chose but others did not goes into the 'hidden' box of the quadrant.

Step 4
Now look at the words that others said about you but you didn't say about yourself. These are things others can see but you can't, so these go in the 'blind-spot' box of the quadrant. This area is fascinating when it comes to increasing your self-awareness, as it will help you see what you currently can't see. It may help explain misunderstandings or different perspectives and reactions. This box will show you where there may be dissonance and what you may want to work on personally.

Step 5
Look at the list of things that you said about yourself but no one else said – these go in the 'hidden' box of the quadrant. There may be good reasons why these things stay hidden; perhaps you wish to keep things private because to reveal them would not be helpful for you or others. Perhaps it is contextual; the present moment may not be the right time to reveal these things to others. Even if that is the case, knowing which parts are hidden from others is useful for you to know.

There may be things in the 'hidden' box that you thought everyone knew and they don't, so you may need to be more deliberate about making those things clear. For example, if you chose 'trustworthy' because this is important to you, but no-one else has chosen that word, you may want to reflect on why that may be. What is stopping them seeing or experiencing this in you? Be mindful at this stage that there may be some different interpretations of vocabulary and some of the disagreements may come down to that, but you will get a sense of whether this is an issue when you see the words.

Step 6
The rest of the characteristics in the list that no one chooses go into the 'unknown' box of the quadrant. There may be characteristics that you want, but you are not there yet and no one else thinks you are either – and that is good to know! These things can inform future training, coaching, reading

CHAPTER 1 THE ONE ABOUT SELF-REFLECTION

and development for you. You can now start being deliberate about pursuing knowledge and experience of these words.

Step 7

Now it is time to draw your boxes! Each of the boxes in the quadrant will be different sizes because of the number of words that are in them – as you draw them you can see your window emerge. This isn't a mathematical exercise, just make sure that where there are more words, there is a bigger 'window'. Let's look at some examples.

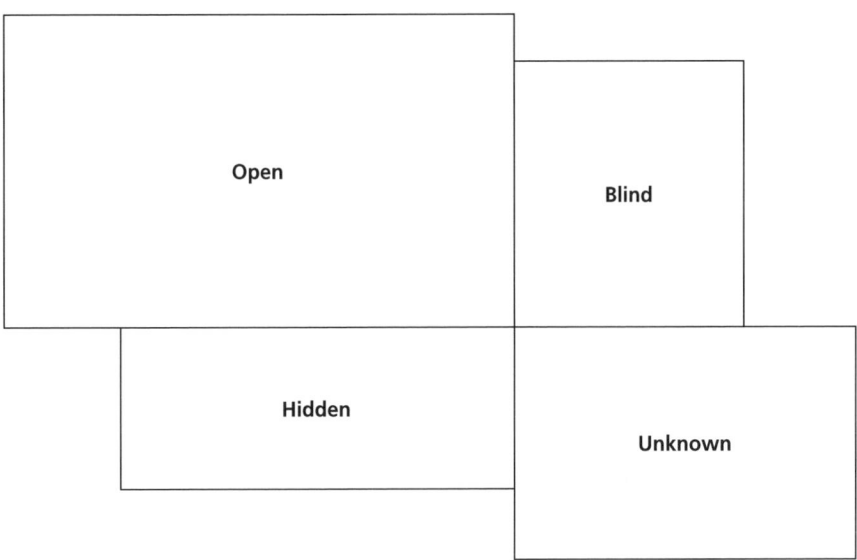

This Johari Window shows a large 'open' box. This person seems to have a good understanding of themselves because it is the same understanding that others have of them. There are still some things in the other three areas, but when the 'open' area is the largest there is probably trust and open communication.

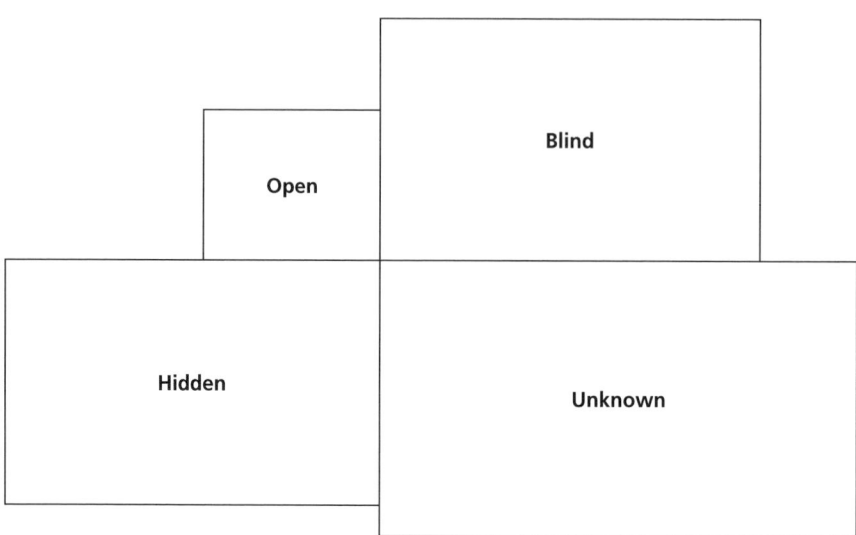

This version may be a newer member of staff, as you would expect the 'open' area to be smaller. There is much that is unknown, but over time the person will want to work on those 'blind' and 'hidden' areas.

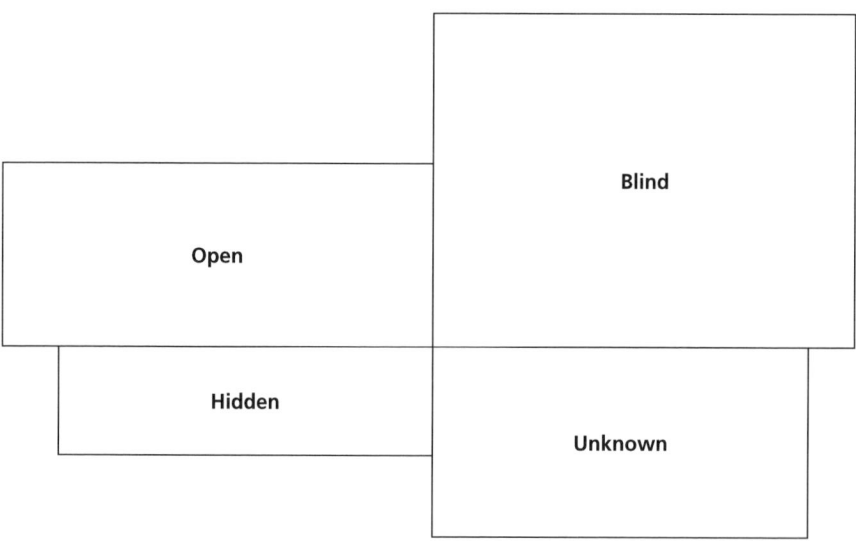

This example is very interesting depending on context. If this is someone who has been in an organisation a while but much of what people say about them is not what they say about themselves, then there is a disconnect. When the 'blind' area is so much larger than the 'open' area, there is some work to do on our own self-awareness. Tools like 360-degree surveys and asking people what they should stop, start or continue doing can help start a conversation. One of the best tools to bring these things into someone's consciousness is through coaching, where people can be asked questions and have the time and space to reflect on themselves and their leadership and behaviours.

The sizes of the boxes impact on personal and professional dynamics, so it can help us work out next steps. This is a personal quadrant; it is for us to decide what we want and need to help us in our own self-reflection. The sizes of the boxes will, of course, change over time, and as the context (and you and your leadership) changes your own Johari Window can help you identify what it is you need to do more, or less, of.

Johari's Window is a tool and like all tools it won't be perfect. It requires us to already have some self-awareness and similar interpretations to others of the adjectives and their meanings. The perception of others may also be skewed, which is why it's important to ensure a number of different people participate in this exercise to give you the most comprehensive view possible.

Stepping out of the box

Identifying where you are and what others think of you is one thing, but doing something with the information is quite another. Here are some things to consider if you want to be more self-aware and create your own change using Johari's Window quadrant:

1. **Open area** – Which words are you really proud of and which ones are you less happy about (even if you agree with your colleagues about the way they describe you)?
2. **Blind-spot area** – Which words are you really pleased about because you are happy people see you in a way that you didn't realise? Which ones do you find surprising and why?
3. **Hidden area** – Which words are there that you wish weren't because you want people to know those things about you? Which characteristics do you not want people to know and why?
4. **Unknown area** – Which of these words do you want to work on and get into the 'open' area in the next few months? How can you deliberately find out?
5. **Opening the window** – What are you going to do to increase the size of the 'open' box and reduce the size of the rest? What could you do to make these things more open?

You could try some of the practical suggestions below to start your move into the 'open' area of the Johari's Window.

1. Try and be more transparent with people about what you think and feel that involves being more honest, more vulnerable and more willing to be open:

    a) Make time as a team to talk about your values and the things that matter. This isn't small talk – it can improve openness, understanding and communication.

    b) Create time to reflect on the last few weeks and give time to explore what you, and your team, are proud of.

    c) Send cards with a message including specific praise, written by you. We get more of the behaviour that we praise and acknowledge, and so whether it is a 'thank you' or a 'thinking of you' card, a birthday or Christmas card – send one. What you comment on, you value, so if you are praising it, people know it is important to you.

2. Ask for more feedback, more regularly. The more you know, the more your 'blind' box decreases:

    a) Ask to meet with someone you trust and ask them to help you understand what is behind the words in the 'blind' area. Ask them for examples so you can see what they are seeing that you are not. It may be that there is a real strength here that, because it comes naturally to you, you haven't ever really acknowledged. This could become a super strength if you were more aware of it and leaned into it more!

    b) Engage in coaching. Some of the 'blind' area characteristics may make you feel uncomfortable because you don't see yourself the way others do. There will be a range of reasons for this, but it is good to unpick this more in a setting where someone can listen and explore it with you.

3. Identify those things that are hidden from others and work out how you can show them to others.

    a) Be deliberate and brave and tell people that you are trying to make something more visible and then ask them how it has gone. For example, 'I am introverted, and this is something that is more hidden from you than I want so I am going to be more deliberate about showing you this part of me. My best thinking is done when I have time set aside to think and to get clear on my thoughts. From now on, for meetings that need it, there will be pre-reading so I can be clear, and we can all reflect before we come to the meeting rather than be rushed to make decisions. I am putting time in my diary to write the pre-reading material.'

   b) After a few meetings have happened, ask people for their feedback. Has it been helpful for them to see the way you think? Are they clearer about how you work and how they can work with you?

4. The Johari's Window will change each time we create one. Put a time in your diary for when you will do another version and spend some time analysing the differences between them. You can't work on everything (and neither should you), so be very deliberate about the areas you want to work on and the characteristic you are hoping will be more open (or less hidden).

Box clever pledge: Self-reflection

My current box is _____ (Date: _____)

I want to be able to be _____ by _____ (date)

I am going to do the following:

1) _____

2) _____

Annotate the quadrant with your own notes. What have you taken away from this chapter?

	Known to self	Not known to self
Known to others	Open area	Blind spot
Not known to others	Hidden area	Unknown

You will find another copy of this quadrant on page 107. Why not put a reminder in your calendar and come back to it in a few months' time and see what has changed?

CHAPTER 2
THE ONE ABOUT CONFLICT

In life and leadership we must handle conflicts, and whether the disagreements are large or small, how we behave in a situation can influence the outcome of it. We need to be problem solvers – even if sometimes we are the only one in the room! As part of conflict management, we become master negotiators, listeners and readers of any situation. We have to think about others and be aware of ourselves so we can push any discussion into a 'problem solving' place. Whether you are in education or business, most of you will not have been trained in how to do this as part of your job.

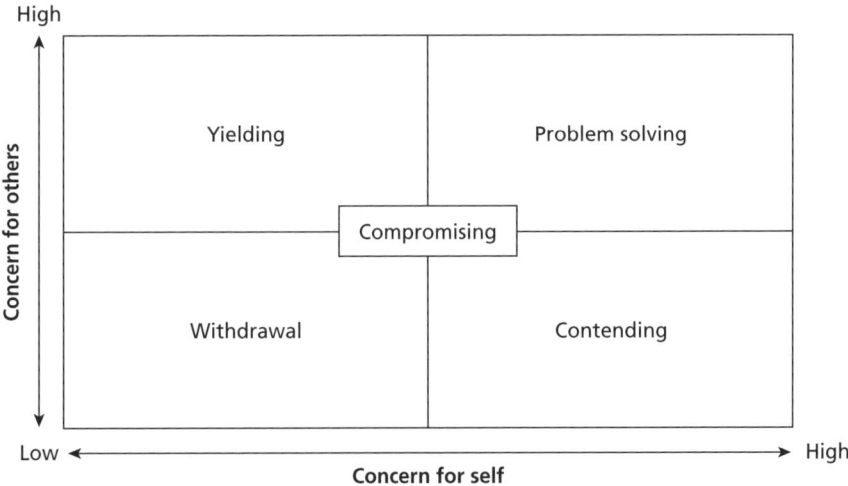

Conflict often plays out in the same way, no matter what the context: two sides with different interests, opinions, priorities and contexts take their positions. One side wants to get the other side to concede defeat, but neither side are willing to move straight away – if at all! Both sides set out their positions and enter into negotiations; if this goes well, after much discussion you may get to an agreement where both sides can just about tolerate some sort of settlement. This may resolve the initial problem, but it often doesn't feel great for either side, and bad feelings and tension often remain until next time – and there usually is a next time. Or, there is a stand-off where neither party will relent and things intensify, escalate and break down. The outcomes are usually win-lose (one side wins and one doesn't) or splitting the difference (compromising). However, the most common outcome is that both lose and things get significantly worse (withdrawal).

The 'approaches to conflict' quadrant helps us to see the different positions we can take. Though there are four boxes, there are five positions:

- Yielding
- Withdrawal
- Contending
- Problem solving
- Compromise

The 'approaches to conflict' quadrant helps us explore all these positions and make an informed choice about where we want to be and the action we can take.

Many conflict and leadership experts believe there is a better way than just settling for win-lose or lose-lose. This approach has different labels such as 'principled bargaining' or 'getting to yes' (Fisher and Ury), but it has worked in countless situations and can work in ours too. Whether the conflict you are in is personal or professional there are techniques we can use to 'get to a yes' or 'avoid a no'. You don't have to explain it to the opposite side, nor even make sure you are playing by the same rules, but we need to be aware of what we are trying to achieve.

Unpacking the boxes: Where am I now?

The five approaches to conflict are formed by whether our concern for ourselves or others is high or low.

Yielding – high concern for others, low concern for self

Sometimes it can look like yielding is the right thing to do, but there are consequences. If you yield, this implies that you have more concern for the interests of others than you have for yourself. In some situations, this may be true and appropriate, but there are some things to check before we take this position:

- Am I yielding because I am people pleasing? Am I trying to avoid disapproval?
- Am I more concerned for others because I struggle to stand up for and express what I really think?
- Am I yielding because I want peace at any cost, even if the cost is me?
- Does yielding just feel easier?

Think of a current conflict and write down all the reasons why you are yielding and then check your motives again. You may choose to stick with yielding, but it is worth assessing what else may be behind this position.

Withdrawal – low concern for others, low concern for self

This position can be discounting, because you are discounting others, and you are discounting yourself through your lack of concern for both parties. There can be some feelings of hopelessness, resignation and defeat with this approach; however, withdrawal can happen for a number of reasons:

- We may be discounting ourselves.
- We may be in a place where we are finding it difficult to discuss an issue.
- We may feel resentful towards others and be lacking in self-confidence.
- We may have a shift in priorities or views and decide that the conflict isn't worth it.

It is worth considering the following questions:

- Why do I have such low concern for others?
- Why do I have such low concern for myself?
- What am I assuming here that could be wrong?
- Has something changed to alter my level of concern for others or myself?

Contending – high concern for self, low concern for others

Contending comes in a number of forms, but it often involves advocating for ourselves at the expense of thinking about others. In this position, we can sometimes become dogmatic, single-minded, arrogant and inflexible. If we are only concerned with ourselves and not with others, we will not get very far in conflict or negotiation. In this position, we give maximum priority to defending our own interests and ignore the interests of others, or we may actively try and hurt or damage others to get what we want.

We can start 'othering' people when we contend, even thinking of them as less than human, which then, in our own minds, justifies our behaviour. We may start using generic labels as a way of othering as we enter into a world of 'them and us', where we exclude and refuse to listen or understand. Empathy is in short supply in this part of the quadrant; we are here to defend ourselves and attack those who challenge us. If we have fallen into this behaviour in a conflict at work, we must ask ourselves:

- Have I started 'othering' in this conflict and what is that doing to my attitude during negotiations?
- Am I still willing to see any other arguments, or have I closed my mind to other opinions?
- How are other people experiencing me in this situation? Is that what I intended?
- What am I fighting for here? Is it to be right or to get the best outcome for the organisation?
- How am I communicating with the other party? Is it through a third party or in emails? Has the lack of face-to-face conversation made 'labelling' and 'othering' easier? We all know how things can be interpreted wrongly or more harshly than intended, but are we willing to behave differently?

Problem solving – high concern for others, high concern for self

Problem solving is, according to many working in the conflict resolution field, the recommended approach. Problem solving requires us to have high concern about ourselves *and* for others, and to find new solutions rather than compromising on what we both want. In this position, we are aware not just of our own feelings, interests, aspirations and needs, but those of others too. As we seek to understand, we are able to create the understanding and will to make changes and find creative problem-solving outcomes. We must find solutions that can benefit both parties.

As we move discussions into the top right corner of the quadrant, we are able to make progress if we establish criteria that identifies what success could look like. How do we do that though? To get into a problem-solving space, we have to ask ourselves:

- Am I able to encourage all parties to think of the purpose of what we are arguing about? What could success really look and feel like without us defining or defending our sides? Can we agree on principles or a big picture?
- Have I genuinely made time to sit with people to discuss and ponder? What would I point to as proof if this is the case?

- After the first move towards problem solving is made, how am I going to keep us there?
- Who are the people on the 'other side' who may be open to this approach? Write their names down and make an effort to understand their concerns.
- What techniques can I use to ensure I am really listening? For example, asking open questions, refusing to interrupt or asking others to expand.

Compromising – balancing the needs of others with the needs of self

Compromising is in the middle of the quadrant because it occupies the mid-point position by balancing the concern for others and self and finding accommodation and possibly even compromise. However, this approach can lead to both parties feeling like this is a lose-lose situation since neither gets all of what they came into the conflict to achieve.

If you can get to a place of compromise, this can work and is certainly better than withdrawal, yielding or contending, which can all make things worse. Sometimes, however, we cannot simply compromise, as doing so could be dangerous or unsatisfactory in the context. In hostage negotiation, for example, the objective is clear, and compromise is seen as 'splitting the difference', which isn't the optimal outcome as Chris Voss makes clear in his excellent book, *Never Split the Difference*. What we can do is listen and try to move people to problem solving where both parties find a way to win, perhaps in a different way to the one they imagined. Win-win is not easy, but it moves us on more effectively in resolving the conflict or disagreement for (hopefully) longer-lasting change.

Stepping out of the box

There are many things that cannot be controlled in conflict resolution, but something that can is the approach you are going to take and how hard you want to work at reaching a problem-solving resolution. Whether the conflict is at work, at home or with friends, the principles are the same: the best chance we have is in compromise or problem-solving approaches. In light of this, here are some questions to consider as you seek to move from the box you are in now to the one you want to be in:

- If you are going to have concern for others and concern for yourself, what do you need to know?
- From your perspective, what are the principles you are arguing over?

- Who are the people, across sides, who may come with you on this approach?

As you move to a problem-solving approach, here are some things you could try:

1. Whatever the conflict is about, establish criteria of what the aim is and work on this together. For example, if we are in an argument with someone about their behaviour, we may agree together on the behaviour criteria for senior leadership before we get into further discussion. If we are arguing with a long-standing stakeholder, we may want to establish the longer-term end goals we are both trying to achieve. Find common ground and work backwards from there. We have to encourage a mentality where all parties (including ourselves!) are prepared to think differently, not defensively.

2. Brainstorm new options that haven't yet been considered so we can start to move away from entrenched positions.

3. Look for joint objectives that neither party can achieve alone and start planning how to make that happen together.

4. Identify those who are committed to problem solving. These innovators and early adopters may work with you early on, and then you can work on the others. Don't worry too much about everyone at this point; work on the people who will take the problem-solving approach and get them onside.

5. It's worth remembering that once you have got both parties into 'problem-solving mode', they have to be kept there. This is not a one off; the work has to continue to happen. Plan dates to meet again, get them in the diary and plan your communication strategy.

6. Ensure you are really listening – get curious, not furious! Ask great questions (perhaps plan them in advance) so you can find out more about the other side. This approach only works if you show concern for others as well as for yourself and get people on to a level where it is not a case of arguing sides but thinking together. 'We', not 'I', is the necessary language here.

7. Check your understanding. Conflict, whether at home or work, often happens when someone has spoken and we haven't really heard what they were saying. Use phrases like, 'I think I heard you say', or 'Can I just play back what I think I have heard?' and always ask, 'Is that right? What have I missed?' Do not assume that you have understood – check that you have. This builds empathy, so people know you are concerned enough about them to really hear.

CHAPTER 2 THE ONE ABOUT CONFLICT

8. To stay in a place where we are concerned for others, we need to be careful of 'othering' or 'generalising', which can creep in frequently. Avoid using the words 'all' or 'everyone', which tend to create tension or arguments. For example, saying 'All the staff feel like this' or 'Everyone is saying the same thing' is going to raise the temperature of the debate unless that is a proven fact with evidence. If we are talking about 'all staff' or 'some people', it is best to name the people because it helps keep us concerned about individuals and stops us making sweeping generalisations. When we use wider terms, we can make the problem sound bigger (or smaller) than it actually is.

Box clever pledge: Conflict

My current box is _____ (Date: _____)

I want to be able to be _____ by _____ (date)

I am going to do the following:

1) _____

2) _____

Annotate the quadrant with your own notes. What have you taken away from this chapter?

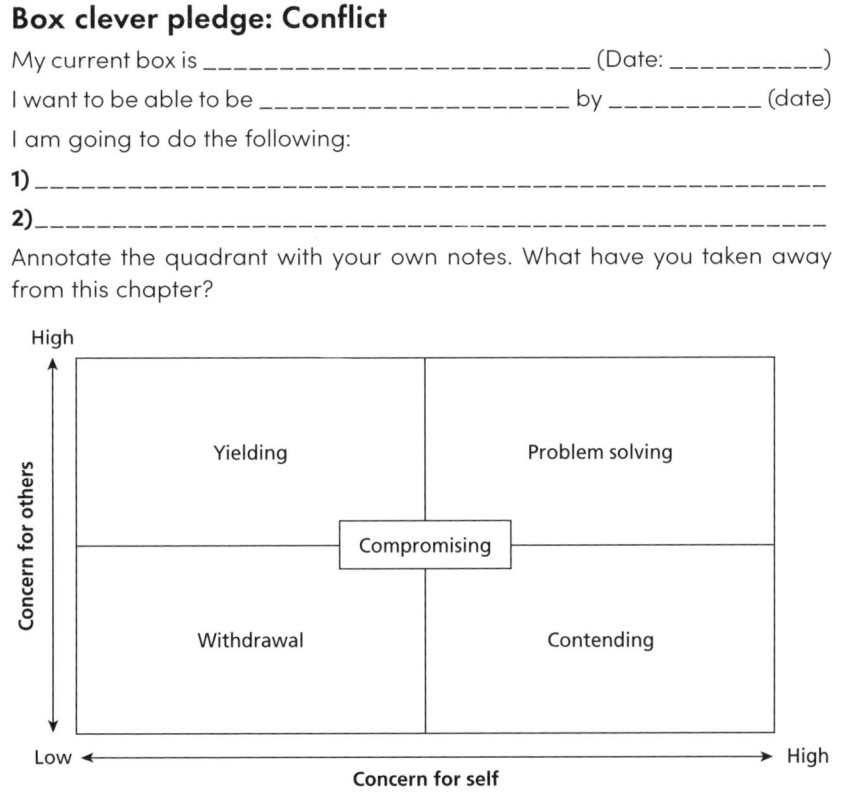

You will find another copy of this quadrant on page 108. Why not put a reminder in your calendar and come back to it in a few months' time and see what has changed?

CHAPTER 3
THE ONE ABOUT SELF-BELIEF AND CHALLENGE

Self-belief is something that is a struggle for many people, and so rather like a pendulum we can swing to the extremes rather than finding balance. If we are too confident, we can be arrogant; if we are not confident enough it can hold us back from taking risks, moving forward and backing ourselves. The sweet spot we have to find is the place between having enough confidence to believe in ourselves and our ability while also having enough humility to embrace that we won't have all the answers and will make mistakes.

People who are genuinely humble are also confident. Why? Because if you are humble, you accept you are fallible and flawed and are relieved of the pressure to try and show the world how perfect you are. Humility is about being grounded – it is about your willingness to be challenged and accept being wrong. This area is often hard for employers to define and assess. There are some consulting firms who are planning to introduce an assessment to identify personality traits including 'sincerity, modesty, fairness, truthfulness and unpretentiousness'. This is nicknamed the 'H factor', which is a combination of 'honesty' and 'humility'.

In this chapter we explore the relationship between confidence, humility, challenge and fear by looking at the work of Adam Grant and Jim Collins. This quadrant illustrates the relationship between our self-belief and our willingness to be challenged.

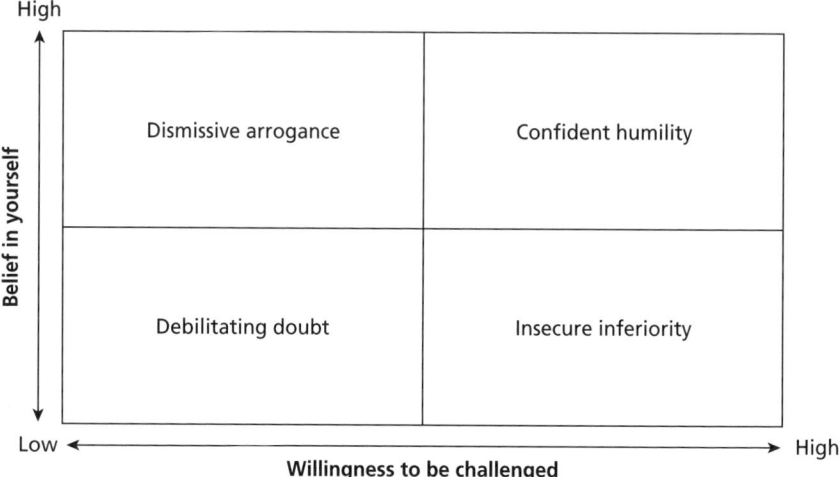

Unpacking the boxes: Where am I now?

Concepts of self-belief and challenge are sometimes hard to make tangible, and although these issues are complex and multi-faceted we can look at what can happen when we are not in the sweet spot between the two.

A reminder at this point: we're talking about places we find ourselves and the attitudes that we display, and both of those things can change. It can be difficult to look in the mirror as there are some things we would rather not see, but great leaders do look at themselves and reflect on where things need to change. There are four main positions we will unpack here.

Dismissive arrogance: High self-belief, low willingness for challenge

This position happens when someone believes in themselves so much that they are unable (or perhaps unwilling) to be challenged by others. Arrogance is a concept that we are familiar with, but the 'dismissive' part deserves particular attention. When people are so confident in their own ability and unable to be challenged, they are not just dismissive of the challenge but are often dismissive of the people who provide it. When we are dismissive, we leave ourselves open to making mistakes as we overestimate our own ability.

Adam Grant and Phil Tetlock, both from Wharton University, outline what happens when we get too over-confident. They argue that there are three modes in which we operate:

- **Preacher** – we are convinced we are right and so we try to persuade everyone else.
- **Prosecutor** – we are trying to prove everyone else wrong.
- **Politician** – we are trying to win the approval of our audience and want to sound like we are right.

Grant and Tetlock (2021) argue that we are missing a mode: the scientist. Scientists favour 'humility over pride and curiosity over conviction'. Scientists look for reasons why they may be right *as well as* reasons why they may be wrong – they are open to both. They want to be challenged, whereas if we are in a place of 'dismissive arrogance', we persuade, persecute or pander to our audience because we believe we are right and we want them to think we are.

As leaders, we can easily slip into this box without always knowing we have done so. The further up the ladder you get, there is a risk that less people tell you the truth. We need to check that our willingness to be challenged hasn't dropped too low. How might we know that? Every now and again it is worth a check of the following:

- When was the last time you admitted to making a mistake?
- When did you last apologise and really mean it?
- When did you last ask for feedback on what you were doing or how you were doing it?
- When was the last time someone challenged you and you took it well?

It's great if we have confidence in ourselves, but let's also ensure we are open to challenge and are willing to hear the critical views and dissenting voices as well as the positive ones.

Debilitating doubt: Low self-belief, low willingness for challenge

This box is an uncomfortable one and many of us will have been there at some point. Where people in the 'dismissive arrogance' box sometimes have more confidence than competence, people in this box may have more competence than confidence because the latter is so low. 'Imposter syndrome' is a phrase that describes people who doubt their ability and their position and therefore lack belief in themselves.

If you feel like an imposter and doubt yourself, you may take longer to offer your opinion or solution, hold yourself back or worry that someone is going to find out that you are not as competent as they think. Although you are willing to learn, your willingness to be challenged may be low. This isn't because you don't want the challenge or don't want to be better (you really do), but rather the impact of being challenged can sometimes feel crushing. If you don't have much belief in yourself and then someone challenges you or picks up on something that isn't quite right, you can find yourself spiralling out of control. In your mind, the small comment becomes something much bigger; you may try to find evidence that you can't do it to justify your view. This now becomes evidence in your mind that you are hopeless and an imposter after all. You now feel you are right, putting you in a vicious cycle of shame, self-blame and paranoia. This is what becomes debilitating.

When we get ourselves in this cycle, everything suffers. Your colleagues may find it hard to provide feedback because of what it may do to you. They can then fall into what Kim Scott (2017) describes as 'ruinous empathy', where they start to care more than they challenge, and it stops them being honest. Feedback is withheld and the repercussions of this can make things worse. You may not seek feedback because your self-confidence can't take the knock you assume will come.

Although others can help you build your self-confidence, it is the work of each individual to do it for themselves:

- Think of a recent time when you have been given feedback – how did you respond?
- Deal with facts. Write down all the evidence that you are good at your job and want to grow. Keep adding to it – the fact you are reading this book can go down as the first piece of evidence!
- Change your language. Start speaking positively about yourself and to yourself.
- What are you assuming that is wrong? If you believed something better and more positive about yourself, what would change?

Roger Jones, a chief executive who helps elevate the performance of executive teams, interviewed leaders and senior executives and identified the same five deep-seated fears. They worried about appearing to be incompetent, vulnerable and foolish; they worried about under-achieving; and they feared political attacks from their colleagues. None of these top-of-mind fears involved the businesses or the organisations they led, but all of them had an impact. The leaders were caught up in themselves, and their fears were limiting their effectiveness. According to Jones' research, the top fears are displayed in problematic ways, such as:

- dysfunctional behaviours
- lack of honest conversations
- too much political game playing
- siloed thinking
- lack of ownership and follow through.

This is the definition of debilitating doubt – it is debilitating leaders as people and will therefore (eventually) debilitate the organisation.

If you doubt yourself, you may also be humble, willing to learn, motivated to work hard and want to do a good job. These are all good things. Be proud of these characteristics and believe in their power but be careful when the doubt grows into something that becomes debilitating.

Insecure inferiority: Low self-belief, high willingness for challenge

Insecure inferiority is similar to but different from debilitating doubt. Whereas those in the left-hand box may find challenge hard to accept because of how it affects them, people in this box are very willing to embrace challenge because they are low in confidence and assume what they are doing is probably wrong anyway.

People in this box may seek out challenge more than normal because they want to get it right so desperately so they can feel better about themselves. This may lead to people criticising themselves in public or making self-depreciating comments to their colleagues, or to quickly make jokes at their own expense so others don't get there first (people may laugh, but it is rarely funny). They may seek challenge constantly because they assume they are not as good as others and want to own the fact they aren't. Perhaps they are insecure in their position or role and feel inferior to those they work with.

This is often the case (and to be expected) when we are new to a workplace, as we don't know much and are learning as we go. However, if these behaviours continue, it can lead to perfectionist tendencies or workaholic behaviour as we constantly seek improvement to be better and feel worthy. Insecure inferiority may also be closely linked with people pleasing, lack of boundaries and an inability to say no (all of which I cover in my two *Time to Think* titles). This is an exhausting pursuit, so it's worth reflecting on what may be driving it:

- Do you assume that everyone else is more competent and doing a better job than you? What impact does this have on you?
- Do you ask for challenge or make jokes about yourself to try and beat others to it?
- If you assumed that you were good at your job and doing well, what difference would this make to you?

Confident humility: High self-belief, high willingness for challenge

This is where we all need to get to, the healthy place of believing in yourself and accepting challenge because you have the humility to know that you need others, are not always right and still have a lot to learn, no matter how accomplished you may already be.

In his book, *Think Again*, Adam Grant says that confident humility can be taught, and outlines studies that have shown the benefits of this approach. One study involved students reading an article on the benefits of admitting what we don't know instead of being certain, and data showed that as a result the odds of them asking for support and help on their areas of weakness went from 65% to 85%. The study also showed the students were more likely to explore different political views to their own and learn from the views of others.

Grant argues that confident humility also improves the quality of both our thinking and *re-thinking*. A study with college and graduate school students showed that those who are willing to revise their beliefs get higher grades; not only that, but students who admit they don't know something get better ratings from both staff and peers and contribute more to teams. There are clear arguments for confident humility being what we should aspire towards.

The 'confident humility' concept is not a new one, but it is something that is being talked about more commonly. In 2022, *Harvard Business Review* published 'Stop Promoting Incompetent Leaders', an article in which they argue that:

> Businesses tend to promote people on the basis of charisma, confidence, and even narcissism. Instead, companies should be putting people in charge who demonstrate competence, humility, and integrity. [...] If you're responsible for assessing leadership candidates, you should work on your ability to distinguish between confidence and competence.

From what I have read and observed, people who sit in the 'confident humility' box:

- Take an interest in others.
- Accept they make mistakes.
- Know they have blind spots.
- Are always wanting to learn and re-think that learning.
- Don't think constantly of themselves.
- Don't think less of themselves.
- Live with less fear because they are at ease with saying sorry.
- Acknowledge their strengths without belittling others.
- Believe they can grow (and want to).
- Are accepting of challenge and feedback (and seek it).
- Have a good relationship with themselves.
- Can be introverts or extroverts – this doesn't depend on personality type.

Getting to, and staying in, a place of confident humility takes deliberate action. It's worth considering the following questions:

- In what ways do you stretch yourself to think and then re-think about what you thought you knew? When do you make the time to do this?
- What is your relationship like with yourself? (Confident humility usually comes from a level of being comfortable in your own mind and body.)
- When things go well in your organisation, who takes the credit? When things go badly, who takes the blame?

Stepping out of the box

Being honest about where you are and where you want to be is a challenge. There is a level of self-awareness required to even work out where you may sit. The Johari's Window exercise in chapter 1 (see page 1) may have brought some of this out, but there are other ways of looking for evidence.

The University of Berkley developed a quiz to ascertain how much 'intellectual humility' a person has. According to their researchers, intellectual humility focuses on recognising the limits of your own knowledge and belief systems and how you handle opposing or conflicting views. When the world seems to be more polarised, we need to have intellectual and confident humility.

You can take this quiz online – it produces a report drawn from three scientifically validated scales aimed to measure intellectual humility (a link is provided on page 121). The statements are as follows:

- Before forming a strong opinion, I prefer to review evidence and different viewpoints.
- I have at times changed opinions that were important to me when presented with new evidence.
- I can recognise the evidence supporting opinions that are different from my own.
- I acknowledge that my beliefs and attitudes may be incorrect.
- I am careful to calibrate the strength of my opinions to the strength of the evidence I have.
- I am willing to admit it if I don't know something.
- I welcome different ways of thinking about important topics.
- Even when I disagree with others, I can recognise that they have sound points.
- I have a hard time admitting when one of my beliefs is mistaken.
- I am willing to hear others out, even if I disagree with them.
- I tend to feel threatened when others disagree with me on topics that are close to my heart.

Whatever your score, there are things you can do to ensure you get into, and then stay in, the 'confident humility' box:

1. When you disagree with someone, ask yourself why you disagree. What is it about the idea or argument that you don't agree with? Ensure you ask yourself where your view came from and then where their view may have come from.
2. When you are struggling to see another point of view, ask yourself, 'What am I missing here?' 'What am I assuming?'
3. Admit when you are wrong and actively seek to change your mind. Adam Fetterman, director of the Personality, Emotion and Social Cognition Lab at the University of Houston, argues that:

    We may refuse to admit we're wrong because we're afraid people are going to look down at us, but, instead, what people like is intellectual humility – that someone is willing to change their opinion when they've heard new information.

    If the facts change, you probably will too!

4. Be information gatherers and be patient. Be very clear with your teams that your opinion may change if the data, facts or context changes. We have to stay flexible and nimble in our thinking and frequently re-think previous ideas. Gather facts to build your confidence if you are struggling – what are you doing well and what evidence is there that you *do* know what you're doing? There will be plenty of evidence, but you need to practice speaking positively to yourself.
5. Practice self-distancing, where you remove focus from 'me' and instead see a situation in the third person. A study in 2021 looking at how to promote intellectual humility and wise reasoning involved participants keeping a diary for one month. The participants used either a first- or third-person perspective in entries that recorded the significant experiences of their days. Results showed that those who had engaged in the third person showed an increase in 'wise reasoning about interpersonal challenges'. Why don't you give this method a try?
6. If you struggle with confidence, uncover the role of nature in reducing internal chatter and negative emotions. The work of psychologist Ethan Kross emphasises the importance of seeking out awe to help us manage chatter and to get perspective, which, in turn, can encourage humility. This feeling is most likely to occur in places that have two key features: physical vastness and novelty. Leave the laptop behind and get outside – it doesn't have to be a day long trek, just a stroll somewhere green!
7. Use Jim Collins' 'windows and mirrors' approach frequently. Confidently humble leaders look out the window to give credit to others when things go well, and if they cannot find a person they credit good luck. At the same time, they look in the mirror to apportion blame and responsibility when things go wrong, never using bad luck as an excuse. This doesn't mean they think they are hopeless – it means they can take responsibility without being defensive.
8. Wherever you are in this quadrant, be very wary of social media and 'comparisonitis'. Comparing our insides to other people's outsides has never been a good strategy and may impact negatively on your confidence and humility. Social media posts are essentially PR tools as they show what people want you to see about them. They do not always reflect the messiness of real life, nor the private struggles people have. If you are struggling for confidence, be careful when you are accessing social media, and if you are very confident, watch you don't get sucked into arguments that require you to dig your heels in and be dismissive of others. Neither will help you or your leadership.

Box clever pledge: Self-belief and challenge

My current box is _____ (Date: _____)

I want to be able to be _____ by _____ (date)

I am going to do the following:

1) _____

2) _____

Annotate the quadrant with your own notes. What have you taken away from this chapter?

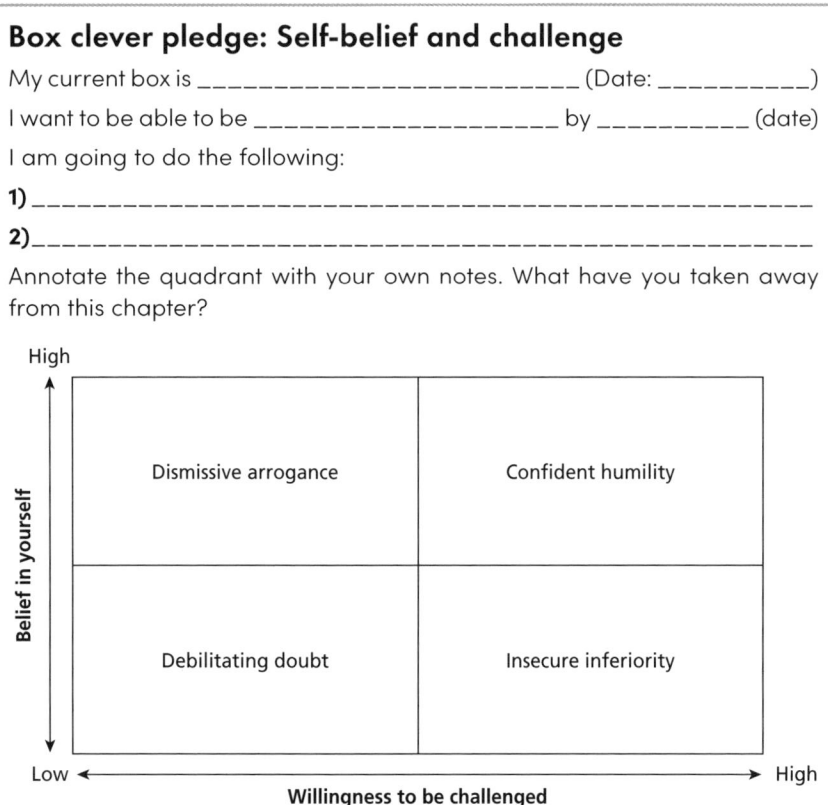

You will find another copy of this quadrant on page 109. Why not put a reminder in your calendar and come back to it in a few months' time and see what has changed?

CHAPTER 4
THE ONE ABOUT BRUTAL FACTS AND HOPE

I wrote about the role of brutal facts and unwavering hope in my book, *Time to Think 1*, because embracing both and getting the balance right is a significant part of being a successful leader. There are consequences if we go too far either way, so by using this quadrant we can understand where we may need to re-balance our approach.

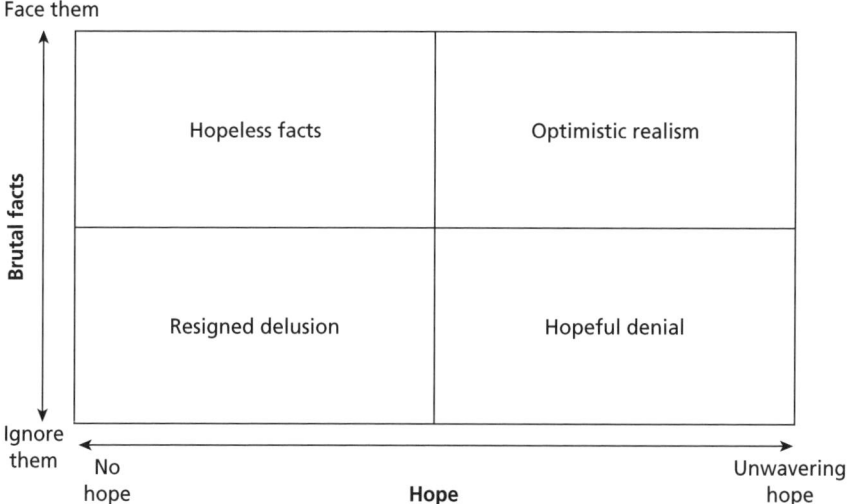

Unpacking the boxes: Where am I now?

It's worth unpacking what we mean by 'brutal facts' and 'unwavering hope' and the difference between hope and optimism, which are often misunderstood and widely debated in academic circles.

Brutal facts

Brutal facts are often hard to take because they probably come with big implications and consequences for you and the people around you. In business, if a company is not profitable year-on-year, that is a brutal fact. If the organisational model is not fit for purpose, you have colleagues who are underperforming, there are redundancies to make or the competition is taking your customers, all of these cannot be ignored. In education or healthcare, if you are seeing a decline in the metrics, more challenging behaviour or a retention and recruitment crisis, these too are brutal facts.

We should neither ignore these facts nor put off addressing them. We should not act rashly, but we do need to start thinking about taking action. No matter how brutal the facts, we should never be brutal in our treatment of people. There is a way to address these facts with empathy, compassion and clarity even if the message may be an unpalatable one for some. It is the facts that are brutal, not our attitude.

Unwavering hope

According to psychologist Richard Lazarus, hope is 'to believe something positive, which does not presently apply to one's life, could still materialise.' Hope is a response to problems, not an avoidance of them. Hope is a positive way of facing challenges if we can identify what the problem is and then paint a picture of what success would look like so that we can tangibly work towards it. It's not 'wishy washy' and it's not just talking a good game; real hope has huge power. As author Rebecca Solnit states, 'hope is not a lottery ticket you can sit on the sofa and clutch, feeling lucky... [it] is an axe you break down doors with in an emergency.'

Hope is not wishful thinking or thinking positive. According to Dr Randy Ross, 'it is a dynamic motivational system tied to inspirational goal setting', and includes positivity, responsibility, agility and reality. Finding hope even in the most challenging situation is what we need to do.

In 2020, a longitudinal study of nearly 13,000 people found that a greater sense of hope was associated with the following:

- Reduced all-cause mortality.
- Fewer chronic health conditions.
- Lower risk for cancer.
- Fewer sleep issues.
- Increased positive mindset.

- Better life satisfaction.
- Maintaining a sense of purpose in life.
- Lower psychological distress.
- Better social wellbeing.

Hope is linked to flourishing, not just physically but also mentally, and many international researchers are conducting studies into the role of hope, compassion and empathy in a range of contexts. It is a more complex topic than one may initially think!

The difference between optimism and hope

Some researchers have concluded that optimism is not the same as hope, and so it's worth defining the differences that are made between the two. Jamil Zaki, author of *Hope for Cynics*, writes that 'optimism tells us things will get better, hope tells us they *could*.' In a study called 'Distinguishing hope from optimism and related affective states', researchers asked participants to define the concepts of optimism and hope and then other concepts such as wishing, desire and joy. They were then asked to write about a time when they had experienced each of these states. What the researchers found is that hope is more closely linked to wishing, although it is different. Researchers also found that 'hope is distinct from optimism by being an emotion, representing more important but less likely outcomes, and by affording less personal control.'

The study defines that hope is when you wish for a positive outcome but are uncertain about what will happen and therefore have little control. Optimism, the researchers argue, is where you have more perceived control and believe in a positive outcome. Both hope and optimism are important and have a role to play. Hope is helpful when we are facing uncertainty, but to convert hope into optimism we need to find a way to gain control to change an outcome.

Hopeless facts: Facing facts with no hope

When we take this position, we may call ourselves realists or pessimists because we see the brutal facts and we can see that the problems we face are enormous. We are not in denial; we clearly see the challenge ahead of us, which is a good thing. However, when faced with these facts we have no confidence nor belief that it is possible to overcome them, or no belief in our own agency to create that change – that is what makes them hopeless facts. When we are in this place (and we have all been there at some point!) there are some things we may notice:

- **We can feel out of control.** We lack agency, belief and a plan, and we can start to feel overwhelmed, which in turn can make us feel stuck. It can also make us ill if we stay here. It may be that your visit to this box doesn't last long, but the impact it has is significant.

- **Hopelessness spreads.** We start talking about the brutal facts (without any hope or plan), which means that other people begin to feel it and we need to manage their reaction to the situation. We start to see people giving up, being disillusioned and morale dropping across the organisation. People talk to each other, despair spreads and it's harder to re-energise people once that starts happening. When people feel their agency has been lost, their motivation soon follows. Only talking about brutal facts without the hope of how things will change can feel very heavy.
- **It can be a wake-up call.** If you are in a job, a relationship or a situation and you get to the point of hopeless facts and know that nothing is going to change, it can catapult you into making a decision. People who know they are in this box and feel they cannot change the situation may decide to instigate their own change. We can start to re-invent or have a phoenix-like rise from the ashes. This can manifest in a range of 'lightbulb' moments, whether that is leaving a job, stepping into a project to try to move things forward or trying totally new things. Sometimes when it feels like all is lost, that is when we find a flickering ember to fan back into a flame.

A temporary visit to this box can be helpful – it can be where the motivation for change can begin. However, staying here for a long period is not good for you or the people you are leading.

Resigned delusion: Ignoring facts and no hope

Although a visit to 'hopeless facts' can help spur us into action, the same cannot be said for 'resigned delusion'. If we find ourselves here, then we are putting a number of things at risk. In this place, we have no hope that anything can or will get better and we are also refusing to see or address the brutal facts, which means things *can't* get better. If we are resigned and hopeless, we are as near to giving up as it's possible to be. There are reasons why we may have taken this position and some questions we should ask ourselves if we get here:

- Have I had a break from work? Have I used my holiday to step away so I can create some distance between me and the situation, so I have a chance to regain some perspective after some sleep and space? This may not seem a very highbrow suggestion, but I would like to guess that people who get into this position have probably not allowed themselves to stop. Sometimes we are simply out of energy and need to stop and recharge. Go home on time (or early!) one night, turn off the laptop, stop the alerts on your phone pinging, get eight hours sleep – do something that helps your mind and body to stop.

- Am I running away from the facts? Is it because I feel shame and it's personally uncomfortable? Is it because I don't know what to do and so can't face it? Is it because I don't know the facts and what is in my head is worse than what the truth may be? The first step here, after you have gained some energy back, is to ask for (or write down yourself) the data-based facts in headline form so you can clearly see the problem. No more hiding from them – sometimes the actual facts are not as bad as the ones we have embellished in our heads.

Sometimes we may find ourselves in a position where we can see the facts, but we have no hope and feel very little power to change anything because other people are refusing to see or address them. It may be that your boss is the one in 'resigned delusion', and so for you to do anything when they lead you is a real challenge. You may not feel you can speak out because there is not a culture where that would be expected or welcomed. You may have weighed up what you know and believe that even if you said something, nothing would change. You may have hope that the facts could change but you have no hope in the people leading you.

These positions are incredibly difficult to handle. Some people whistle blow, some leave or some stay but resign themselves to the situation. Others keep trying to speak up and hope for a breakthrough but risk alienation. If people in your organisation are 'managing' you because you cannot see the reality, you have an even bigger problem.

As leaders, we must listen to those working with and for us. If we are at risk of not even seeing the facts, we have to make sure that we don't miss them. We have to show staff that we are tackling stubborn problems if they can see them in plain sight. We may have to ask staff openly (and perhaps even confidentially) to tell us what we may be blind to. That could mean asking them to:

- Complete staff surveys so we can take the temperature.
- Compile a 'frustrations list' of the things that are stopping people doing their job as well as they would want to.
- Give us feedback, whether that is a 360-degree survey or another tool.

We have to build in opportunities to listen, ask the right questions and show we are responding to what we hear.

Hopeful denial: Ignoring facts but unwavering hope

Although this box may look and feel a little better than the previous two, it isn't. If we are in this box, we may find ourselves in the realm of 'toxic positivity' and wishful thinking. Here is where we need to make a very clear distinction between hope and optimism. We can desire, want, wish and hope all we want; we can be cheerful and sound positive, but if we are ignoring the reality of the situation it's unlikely anything will change, and people will stop believing us. In this box, it looks like we are in control, but we are not. If we don't have a plan because we haven't faced the facts, we are not in control.

Having hope will help you endure, but it's likely that when you eventually have to face the facts or see the obstacles, disillusionment can set in. That is what happened to the prisoners of war who were captured along with Jim Stockdale, as told by Jim Collins in *Good to Great*. Jim Stockdale had a belief that he would eventually be released from prison, but he faced the facts that this was an open-ended situation with no timeline. Facing that fact made him an optimistic realist. The other prisoners had an unrealistic optimism that release would happen soon – that belief was based on a hope, want and a wish. When they eventually had to face the brutal fact that they were not going to be released soon, it was too much for them and they died of broken hearts.

There are clear risks of being in positive denial:

- If others see the facts that you are ignoring, you are going to look out of touch.
- Toxic positivity in the face of brutal facts will damage your leadership and the trust of your teams or organisation. You also risk irritating people because there is a gap between your positivity and their reality.
- Brutal facts will reveal themselves eventually – ignoring them doesn't make them go away.
- You don't have to admit brutal facts to all of your organisation – sometimes that isn't appropriate – but if you are not facing reality you are putting others, and your organisation, at risk.
- Good decisions cannot be made when facts are ignored. No amount of talking positively changes brutal facts.
- We may be denying ourselves. It is highly likely that something in you is telling you something isn't right, but you're trying to bury the niggle and hope it will all be ok – this can have a detrimental impact on our mental

and physical health. We do this at work and we can do it at home. In a recent television advert, the NHS have produced an advert asking people to take action if they notice the smallest symptoms that could be related to cancer and urging them not to excuse it away. Many of us find it easier to excuse it away and hope it is nothing, rather than deal with what it could be. Hope is not a strategy here – it won't change the facts that need addressing.

We sometimes have an 'optimism bias', where we overestimate how much we can achieve, or a 'confirmation bias', where we seek out facts that will confirm our own view while dismissing any contrary evidence. If both biases are at play, we are not grasping the truth and will eventually have to deal with the consequences. Perhaps we simply say, 'I'm sure it will be fine', yet fail to be convinced of our own words.

What are you dealing with today that you know but are trying to 'unsee' or 'unfeel'? Ask yourself one simple question: 'What are the consequences of me trying to pretend this isn't happening?'

Optimistic realism: Facing facts and unwavering hope

This is where we need to be; it was where Jim Stockdale was. Like him, if we face reality and we are optimistic, we have some control and a plan that we believe is likely to address the issues. Realism is when we accept a situation as it is and are prepared to deal with it; it is rooted in evidence, rationality and logic. Optimism is when we have confidence about the future and some control over how we will bring it about. If we live out our lives and our leadership in optimistic realism, it doesn't mean that everything will work out perfectly, but researchers in this field have identified some interesting patterns emerging for optimists:

- Being an optimist won't make outcomes better if they are out of your control, but it will help you deal with them without becoming stressed.
- Optimists are problem-solvers who try to improve any situation they find themselves in.
- If the situation can't be changed, optimists are more likely than pessimists to accept that and then move on.
- Scheier, one of the leading researchers in this area, states that optimists are more likely to engage in behaviours that protect them from disease and help them recover from illness. They are less likely to drink, smoke and have unhealthy diets, and are more likely to sleep well and exercise.
- Optimists are more resilient in the face of extreme events.

- Optimism is contagious! When we are in the company of someone who is an optimist, we can feel energised and positive and then start to believe that we can improve too. It's why listening to inspirational keynotes, podcasts or reading books can be so helpful to us.
- Optimism is good for us and the people around us.

If you are an optimistic realist, you probably have what Scheier and Carver call 'dispositional optimism'. This is when we possess a general expectation that things will work out well for us, no matter what the situation. It is an attitude that helps you take measured risks, work towards an end goal and also helps you enjoy greater wellbeing. Jim Stockdale is a great example of 'dispositional optimism' – he was not defeated by his circumstances, rather he was optimistic but also realistic.

Stepping out of the box

It is likely that we journey around this quadrant frequently, depending on the situation and perhaps even how much sleep we have had. Being an optimistic realist and having 'dispositional optimism' is a necessary tool for healthy leadership. Whether you call it hope or optimism is a very live academic debate but what we need involves positivity, responsibility, agility and reality.

You may not know if you are an optimist or not. Although tests to measure optimism can be blunt tools, they are quick and helpful for us to see where we may be and to help us step out of where we are and into where we need to be. There is a test called the Life Orientation Test (LOT) which was written by Scheier, Carver and Bridges in 1994 and is used widely.

To do the test, you answer the questions using the following scale to indicate the extent of your agreement:

0 – Strongly disagree

1 – Disagree

2 – Neutral

3 – Agree

4 – Strongly agree

Be as honest as you can and try not to let your response in one question influence your response to the others. There are no right and wrong answers.

1) In uncertain times, I usually expect the best.
2) It's easy for me to relax.

3) If something can go wrong for me, it will.
4) I'm always optimistic about my future.
5) I enjoy my friends a lot.
6) It's important for me to keep busy.
7) I hardly ever expect things to go my way.
8) I don't get upset too easily.
9) I rarely count on good things happening to me.
10) Overall, I expect more good things to happen to me than bad.

How to score: ignore your responses to statements 2, 5, 6 and 8 – these are only there as fillers to obscure the purpose of the test and are not scored. Statements 1, 4 and 10 are the ones that measure optimism, so simply add up the scores of these three. Statement 3, 7 and 9 are reverse code items, meaning they are negative. For these three you need to reverse the scores, so 1=3, 2=2, 3=1, 4=0. For example, if you gave the statement a 4, give yourself 0. Add these up to get a total score. Now add both subtotals together to get your optimism score. A score of less than 13 indicates low optimism, 14–18 moderate optimism and 19–24 high optimism.

Whatever your score is, what do you need to do to be an optimistic realist? Here are some ideas to try:

- Find someone who is an optimistic realist and spend more time with them, observing how they tackle certain issues.
- Surround yourself with opportunities to see and feel optimism that is grounded in reality, whether that is listening to a keynote, a podcast, attending a conference or reading a book.
- Sometimes we chase the big change and then lose hope when it doesn't happen quickly enough, and then we find ourselves in a different box. Optimistic realists want to see results and change but also continue to believe that we have more agency than we think and that we can be agile and responsive. Sometimes we must be patient and know that whatever obstacles we face, we will find a way round – that is what optimists do.

Box clever pledge: Brutal facts and hope

My current box is _____ (Date: _____)

I want to be able to be _____ by _____ (date)

I am going to do the following:

1) _____

2) _____

Annotate the quadrant with your own notes. What have you taken away from this chapter?

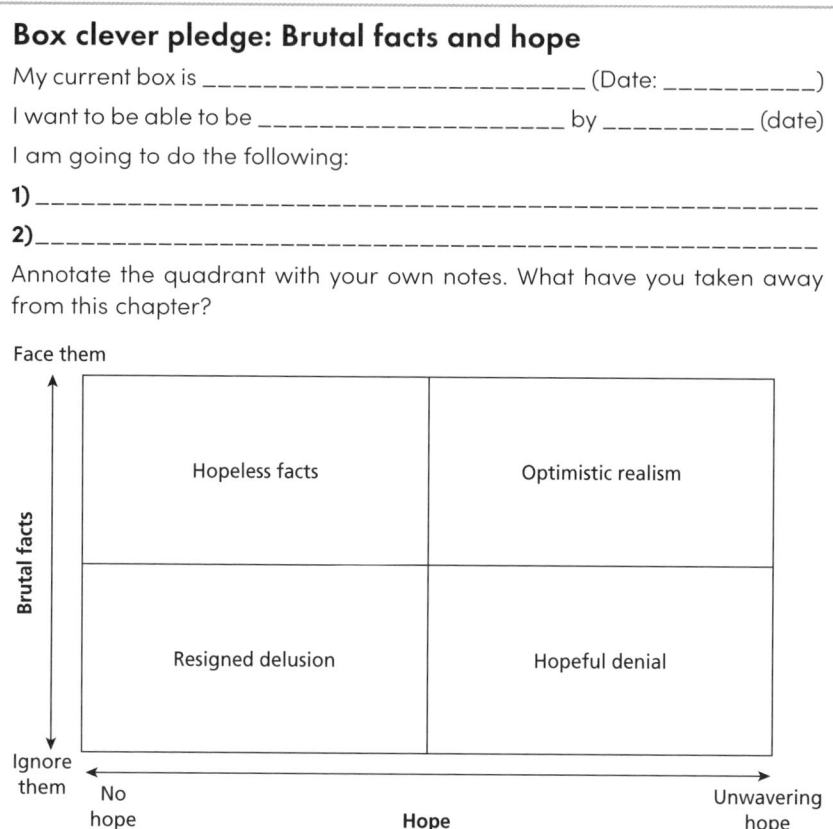

You will find another copy of this quadrant on page 110. Why not put a reminder in your calendar and come back to it in a few months' time and see what has changed?

CHAPTER 5
THE ONE ABOUT FULFILMENT AND BOUNDARIES

We sometimes say to people we love, 'I just want you to be happy.' I wonder if that's what we really mean. I prefer the word 'fulfilled', which means being content, gratified or satisfied because of fully developing one's abilities and character. If we are able to create boundaries in our lives and are able to enforce them, we get a degree of balance that can lead to fulfilment. We don't always find the balance between being fulfilled and having boundaries, and when that happens we notice something about our behaviour that we shouldn't ignore, it can be a tell for us that something needs to change. It may not even be us who sees it, but the people closest to us.

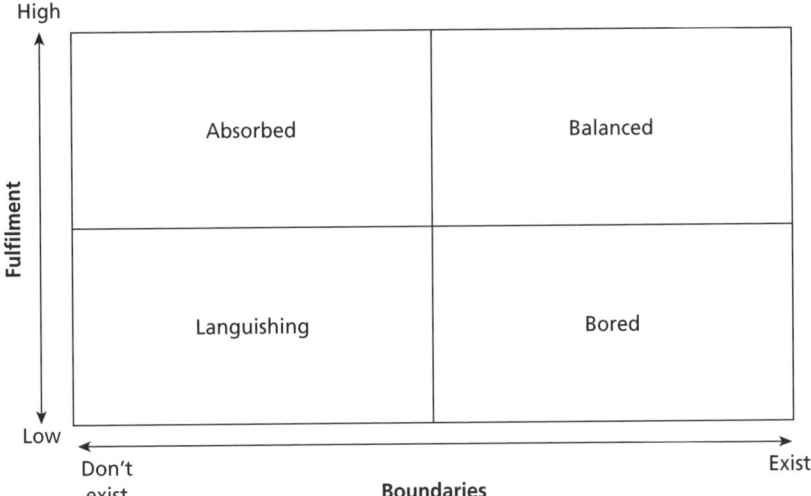

Unpacking the boxes: Where am I now?

Our relationship between boundaries and fulfilment is an interesting thing to think about. Both areas are crucially important for us as humans and as leaders. Fulfilment in work is a wonderful thing. If you are fulfilled in your job, it's highly likely that these statements are true for you:

- You are in flow regularly.
- You are learning new things rapidly.
- You are performing confidently.
- You believe in the organisation's mission.
- You enjoy working with your colleagues.
- There is the right level of challenge.
- You feel valued and supported.
- You feel your contribution is important.
- You can see the influence you are having.

To flourish, we need to feel all of these things to one degree or another.

Boundaries are also important. We need to know what we want and what we don't want, personally and professionally, and be able to say 'no' and have agency and autonomy over our own lives. We need to be able to stop and ensure that we know what it is we want.

What happens when we fall out of the sweet spot of being fulfilled and having boundaries? None of these positions are 'wrong' or 'right' – we all find ourselves moving between positions. What is interesting is recognising why you are there and what has changed or needs to change.

Absorbed: High fulfilment and no boundaries

If you feel fulfilled at work, congratulations! It's likely that the list above is your lived reality, and that is a gift. However, when we are in the 'absorbed' box it usually means that fulfilment may be coming at a cost. We can be so fulfilled that everything else in our life pales into insignificance, and boundaries that we chose (or had to 'choose'!) are long crossed. This is often a choice of course, but it's worth reflecting on whether this is deliberate or a change has crept up on us.

Sometimes we need to go into the 'absorbed' box. When an organisation is going through change, it may need you to do more than normal and work longer than usual. If there is an important inspection or deadline, sometimes we sacrifice our time and boundaries to get the job done. If you are fighting for your organisation's existence or something happens that challenges its stability, then you want to do everything it takes. We have all tipped into 'absorbed' because the job demands it, and that is normal (and even expected), but we shouldn't live there permanently.

When we start living in this box for long periods of time without boundaries but utterly absorbed, we risk overworking and underliving. We may not see the issue, but other people around us often do. There are some common things that happen to our behaviour in this box – the list is a sobering one:

- We don't turn off devices in case we are needed by work.
- On holidays, we are thinking about work or using the time to work despite the fact we said we wouldn't.
- We say 'yes' to things we should be saying 'no' to.
- We stop investing in other important relationships in our lives because of the job.
- We struggle to stop and walk away.
- We start 'phubbing' (phone snubbing), where we check our work phones and don't listen to anything people are saying to us.
- In time, we may be addicted to this level of all-absorbing working.
- We may link our identity to our job, and our worth to our productivity.

In her book, *Women Who Work Too Much* (and it isn't just women!), Tamu Thomas calls this behaviour 'toxic productivity', where we start to become addicted to productivity and can't (or won't) stop. Although this may be our choice for a period of time, we must think about the example this is setting to other colleagues. If you are the leader of the team and are working like this, how do you think your team feels? Our colleagues are watching, and they take their lead on what is expected of them from us. We may have started overworking and being absorbed because the organisation needed it, but if the threat has reduced, are we still working like it hasn't?

You should ask yourself:

- What was the threat and is it still requiring me to work like this?
- What are the consequences of remaining absorbed?
- Have I become addicted to the feelings of productivity?
- What is my exit plan from this place?
- If I am going to stay here for a little longer, what do I need to put in place to ensure that this is manageable?

- In 15 years' time, will future me have any regrets over the way I am working now?

You may ask yourself all these questions and find that being absorbed is still the right choice for you and for your organisation. It is, however, always worth checking it is.

Languishing: Low fulfilment and no boundaries

Where the 'absorbed' box may make us feel good (which, in part, is why we're willing to break our own boundaries), the 'languishing' box is very different. If we gain low or no fulfilment from work and yet also have no boundaries, we may well feel resentful of the people we work with and for. Although there may be valid reasons for this, we are ultimately the ones who set our own boundaries.

When we exist in this box, we are possibly being asked to do more and more; it may not be fulfilling for us, so we are probably unhappy and may also feel we are not able (or willing) to say no. Those who feel like this often leave work through choice or burnout. If you are in this box, then you don't feel like you are flourishing.

Dr Corey Keyes (2022) describes languishing as a 'state of being that is characterised by a lack of vitality or zest for life, and a sense of stagnation and emptiness.' It's a condition where a person can function adequately but lacks a sense of fulfilment. In his book, *Languishing*, Dr Keyes outlines some of the symptoms you may experience:

- You feel emotionally flattened.
- A sense of inevitability has washed over you.
- You find yourself procrastinating at work.
- More and more things strike you as being irrelevant, superficial or boring.
- You feel disconnected from your community.
- Your job feels pointless in the grand scheme of things.
- Small setbacks make you feel defeated.
- You find yourself being steamrolled by others with strong opinions.
- You don't know what you are doing well and what you should improve.

Recognising that this is what you feel is the first step, and there are things we can do to move into 'flourishing' which we will explore in the 'Stepping out of the box' section (see page 46).

Bored: Low fulfilment but boundaries exist

Being bored can be frustrating or liberating depending on your context. You may choose to be in a job that doesn't fulfil you because you want boundaries in place and that is the compromise. Many people take a different job when their personal circumstances change because their priorities have changed; they may opt to step down out of leadership or to go part-time. Others would rather be bored over being stressed or working long hours. If this is a deliberate choice, that may well be the box you need and want to stay in. You have boundaries, and they are likely to have been fought for and are therefore important to you.

If you have boundaries but are also bored when you don't want to be, this is a different issue entirely. You may feel you can do more and contribute more and are frustrated. You may find what you are doing demoralising because it isn't challenging enough for you. You may find yourself in a leadership position that is very senior and yet be doing work that doesn't make you come alive, as you are not absorbed or fulfilled. You wouldn't be alone if you felt like this; according to a Gallup poll (2024), the rate of global employee engagement is at 23%. This is the highest rate of engagement since Gallup began measuring it, and it still feels woefully low. According to their report, 62% of employees are not engaged and 15% are actively disengaged. The UK fares particularly badly compared to the US – 90% of UK workers do not feel enthusiastic about their work or their workplace and 60% are 'quiet quitting'. Unfortunately, this makes the UK the most dissatisfied and disengaged workforce in Europe.

We don't have to remain in this box though, even if our job doesn't change. But if you are unfulfilled at work, what can you do? Consider the following:

- **Decide what you want now.** According to research by Yale professor Amy Wrzeniewski, people fall into three categories: work as a career, work as a job and work as a calling. Knowing what you want work to be can help your expectations.
- **See if parts of your job can be customised.** It may be that you would feel fulfilled if you could add one thing to your role that brings you real joy. Your workplace will benefit and you feel more engaged – they keep you and you feel fulfilled. It's worth thinking what could be added or amended – have that conversation. It may not take a big change, just a tweak.
- **Think about a 'side hustle'.** You may decide that there is nothing you can change about being unfulfilled at work, but you find something outside of work that excites you and brings you fulfilment. Not all of us will find

what we are looking for in the workplace, so why not look outside of it? Is there another place where you can engage to find fulfilment?

- **Be honest about the trade-off.** Be clear with yourself that you are choosing to be less fulfilled at work so you can have the boundaries that you want.
- **Pay attention to what you pay attention to.** What are the parts of your job that you really love and feel fulfilled by? Think carefully about who it's with, what you are doing, how you are doing it and when you are doing it. What does this show you about where you are fulfilled? It may be that you can tap into something that you hadn't even realised really mattered to you.

Balanced: High fulfilment and boundaries exist

Though there are times in life when being in another box for a little while is necessary, I would imagine most of us want to spend the majority of our time being both fulfilled and having boundaries so we can avoid overworking and underliving. People who are fulfilled are personally engaged and professionally supported. According to Dr Keyes, flourishing happens when we feel:

- Happy, interested and satisfied with life.
- We have something important to contribute to society.
- We belong to a community.
- That people are basically good.
- That our society is becoming a better place for all people.
- That the way our society works makes sense to you.
- That you like most parts of your personality.
- That you are good at managing the responsibilities of your daily life.
- That you have warm and trusting relationships with others.
- That you have experiences that challenge you to grow and become a better person.
- That you are confident to express your own ideas and opinions.
- That your life has a sense of direction and meaning to it.

We don't have to score highly on all of these areas, but we do need a number of them to be present in our lives to feel that we are flourishing.

In *Languishing*, Dr Keyes provides a questionnaire that helps us measure our level of 'flourishing'. He argues that we don't need to tick every box, every day

CHAPTER 5 THE ONE ABOUT FULFILMENT AND BOUNDARIES

– we need to have at least one from the emotional wellbeing section box and at least six from the social and psychological wellbeing sections.

Criteria for flourishing						
During the past month how often did you feel	Never	Once or twice	About once a week	Two or three times a week	Almost every day	Every day
Emotional wellbeing						
1. Happy	0	1	2	3	4	5
2. Interested in life	0	1	2	3	4	5
3. Satisfied with life	0	1	2	3	4	5
Criteria for flourishing: Can you circle 4 or 5 in response to at least one of these first three questions?						
Social wellbeing						
4. That you had something important to contribute to society	0	1	2	3	4	5
5. That you belonged to a community (social group, school, neighbourhood, etc.)	0	1	2	3	4	5
6. That our society is a good place or is becoming a better place for all people	0	1	2	3	4	5
7. That people are basically good	0	1	2	3	4	5
8. That the way our society works made sense to you	0	1	2	3	4	5
Criteria for flourishing: Can you circle 4 or 5 in response to at least six of the questions above and below? (Since both social and psychological wellbeing are a measure of healthy functioning, high marks in either category can meet the criteria for flourishing)						
Psychological wellbeing						
9. That you liked most parts of your personality	0	1	2	3	4	5
10. That you were good at managing the responsibilities of your daily life	0	1	2	3	4	5

Criteria for flourishing						
During the past month how often did you feel	Never	Once or twice	About once a week	Two or three times a week	Almost every day	Every day
11. That you had warm and trusting relationships with others	0	1	2	3	4	5
12. That you had experiences that challenged you to grow and become a better person	0	1	2	3	4	5
13. That you are confident to express your own ideas and opinions	0	1	2	3	4	5
14. That your life has a sense of direction or meaning to it	0	1	2	3	4	5

Being in the 'balanced' box means you can feel fulfilled without it taking over your whole life; you can love your job and also balance it with the rest of your life. We can work and we can live, it's not one or the other – it's both. We are in control of where we put our time and energy – it's not in control of us.

Stepping out of the box

At different seasons of our life, we are in different areas of the quadrant. Knowing where you are and why you are there can help you feel in control. Here are some questions to ask yourself about your current position:

1. Are you comfortable with where you are in the quadrant right now? Why are you there? Does this work for you? What do your closest friends and family think?
2. Are you overworking and underliving? What is the impact of this on you, your workplace and your loved ones?
3. What do you find energising? Is there enough of that in your life now? If the answer is 'no' at work, what could you do outside of work to enable this to happen?
4. If you struggle with boundaries, which of them do you keep crossing? What are the consequences of doing so?

CHAPTER 5 THE ONE ABOUT FULFILMENT AND BOUNDARIES

5. Of all the areas of the quadrant, which two areas do you alternate between? How do you know when you need to move into another area deliberately? For example, there may be a certain cycle in your work that means you have to step into 'absorbed' for a short period of time. There may be other times when being in 'bored' for a little while is actually helpful.

Box clever pledge: Fulfilment and boundaries

My current box is _____ (Date: _____)

I want to be able to be _____ by _____ (date)

I am going to do the following:

1) _____

2) _____

Annotate the quadrant with your own notes. What have you taken away from this chapter?

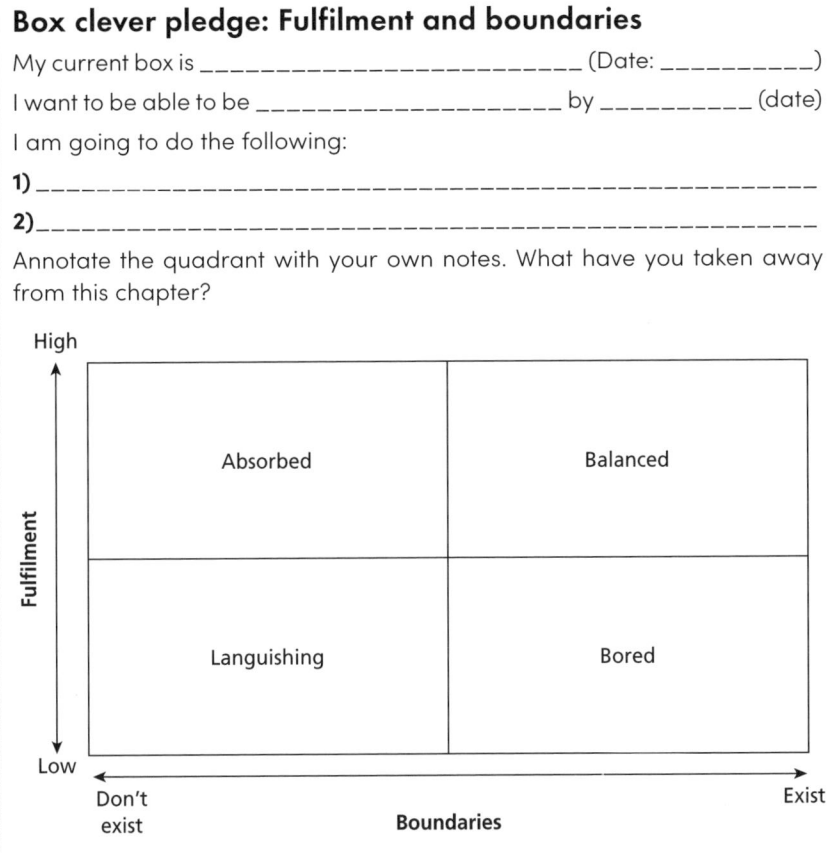

You will find another copy of this quadrant on page 111. Why not put a reminder in your calendar and come back to it in a few months' time and see what has changed?

CHAPTER 6
THE ONE ABOUT IDENTITY

In his book *Mojo: How to Get It, How to Keep It, How to Get it Back When You Lose It*, leadership coach Marshall Goldsmith explores the building blocks of 'mojo'. One of those building blocks is identity – who do you think you are?

Who we think we are is an important question that Goldsmith argues people often find hard to answer. Perhaps it's because we don't know where to look for an answer, or we don't really understand the question. Do I answer with:

- My beliefs and opinions?
- How I was brought up?
- What others say I am?
- Who I want to be?
- Who I think I am now?
- What I used to be?

Goldsmith describes the 'tug of war' that can exist in our own minds as we think about all of these questions. Ultimately, there is tension between what we were and what we want to be, and how we see ourselves and how others may see us. If we want to move ourselves into the future, we need to be aware of the interplay between these four positions.

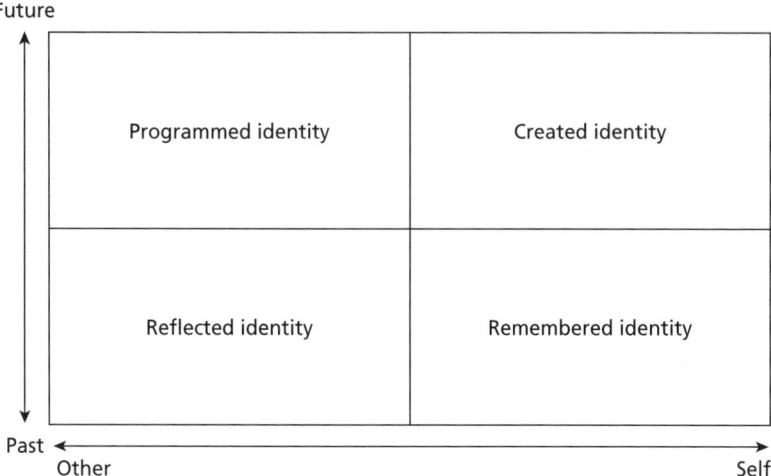

Unpacking the boxes: Where am I now?

Identity is a complex topic, but this quadrant can help us start to think about how our identity has been formed and how we can update the story if we are being held back. Goldsmith suggests that each of the four boxes are different sources of our identity and, combined, they influence our mojo. He defines mojo as 'that positive spirit toward what we are doing now that starts from the inside and radiates to the outside.'

Programmed identity: Where the future and the opinions of others collide

This identity is created from people sending messages to us about who we are or what we will become in the future. We may have been told from an early age by our caregivers that we are intelligent, funny, hardworking or organised. We may have been told the opposite, and it has had a very different impact. It's not just our families who tell us these things – programmed identity can be influenced by our teachers, our profession, the culture we grew up in, the company we work for or the friends we keep. Each of these things shape our identity when we are programmed to behave a certain way. It is worth asking ourselves:

- Is the programmed identity I was given serving me well?
- What would I keep and what would I want to reprogramme?
- What kind of programming am I doing with others?

There are two interesting things about programmed identity: it can change, and it can be blamed.

It can change
Many companies pride themselves in 'programming', and it can be an important part of the culture and identity of a company. For example, if you enter the British Armed Forces there is a new identity on offer, a new way of seeing yourself and working with your colleagues, who will become a tight knit group. They want to create a social identity where there is a shared sense of 'us' by embodying who they are and what they want to be – it is a new programmed identity. Indeed, research with the Royal Marines (Peters and Haslam, 2018) showed that trainee officers were more likely to emerge as leaders and be recognised as such when they acted in ways that showed their interest in the group's collective goals.

The British Army website states that the leaders act as, 'an identity impresario, creating, sustaining, or embedding structures that allow group members to enact their social identity.' This new programmed social identity is seen in their regimental colours, customs, parades, community events and wreath-laying ceremonies such as Remembrance Sunday. For them, it really matters.

This can happen in a range of professions, not just the British Armed Forces, and can be a positive and powerful change for individuals and teams.

It can be blamed
Programming can also be used as an excuse. We may blame our parents for the way we behave or blame the place in which we were raised for our limited understanding on wider societal issues. We may even blame the organisation we work for or claim a helplessness that we feel has been programmed into us. For example, when people come out of the army and find adjusting to civilian life hard, they may blame the very programming that made them.

However, there is only so far this blame game will go before we are made to face up to the fact that using any 'programmed identity' as a scapegoat for our behavioural mistakes isn't going to help us improve. If, for example, we have an arrogant streak because our parents have told us we are the most intelligent person on the planet and everyone else is jealous of us, people at work may not respond well. We can blame our parents or workplace for programming us this way, but ultimately we have to take responsibility and change our programming if we know that it needs to change. If we don't, we can easily find ourselves feeling like victims and being stuck.

Reflected identity: Where the past and other people's opinions collide

Goldsmith argues that reflected identity is 'where the past and other people's opinions meet.' This identity is formed through feedback. People may remember something in your past and remind you of it, or a work colleague tells you how you are being perceived. You may not recognise this version of you, but it becomes a reflected identity; this can also be positive or negative. The right kind of feedback may give you confidence and help you see yourself in a positive light.

Other people may paint a reflected identity that catapults you back to someone you used to be (and not who you are now or you want to be in the future). This can often happen when we see people from earlier in our careers (or from our school days) and their view of us then is not who we are now. Their view may be based on faded memories, gossip or their own perceptions. You may agree with what they say about that time in your life, but that doesn't mean it is who you are now.

Ask yourself the following questions:

- What is the feedback that I remember getting that is no longer who I am?
- Which parts of the reflected identity are trying to take me back to the past?

Remembered identity: Where the past and self collide

This box combines what we know about ourselves with the things we remember from our past. These are the touchstones (some bad and some good) that have had an influence on us. When we tell other people about ourselves, eventually these are the things that are likely to get a mention. This remembered identity may have given you your views on your strengths and weaknesses. We may hear people who are well into adulthood saying, 'I was never any good at maths at school' or 'when I was a teenager, I wasn't very confident' – both of these statements may not bear any resemblance to who you are now.

Ask yourself the following questions:

- What touchstones from my past show how much I have changed?
- Does the picture of me in the past resemble myself anymore? (Sometimes we can cling to those touchstones even though we are now a different person.)

Created identity: Where self and future meet

This is the identity that *we* decide for ourselves. This identity is not controlled by the past or by other people – it's created by us now and can be very liberating. We can change because our role needs it or our leadership requires it, but as our identity changes so does our behaviour.

It's possible to reinvent and reshape our identity. We may not have been creative at school, but that doesn't mean we can't be now. We may have been told we weren't organised enough in a previous job, but that doesn't mean we can't be organised now. In this box, we need to be very aware of where we are limiting ourselves through our own attitudes. Just because we weren't a certain way in the past, that doesn't mean we can't be like this now. Some leaders I work with fear that people who they know from the past may say, 'You've changed'. My response to that is, 'Good, I hope they do say that. What's the alternative, them saying, "You haven't changed since you were 12?" Is that really any better?' At some stage in created identity, we have to decide who and what we want to be.

'Created identity' isn't about playing dress up and pretending to be someone else – it's about deciding who we want to be and then learning new things, having new experiences and being open to personal change. You have a bigger capacity for change than you probably realise. Whether you want to create a new identity for yourself or rediscover elements of you that you have lost, it's possible to change.

Ask yourself the following questions:

- Who do I want to be now and in the future? What are the first steps in becoming that?
- I can change; I have already. What are some of the ways that I have already changed in the last few years?

Stepping out of the box

Many of us find it challenging to step away from what we have been told and the things that have been said about us. Many of those things will be positive but may still cause us problems. Being told 'you're bright' or 'you never give up, you just keep going' may prevent us from admitting we are stuck. Some of the things we have heard and 'locked in' our heads and hearts will be negative and will be preventing us from being the person we want to be now.

What can we do when we want to start moving into the 'created identity' box? Here are some things to try. They can work for you but can also work for your teams.

For you:

- Write down what you want to be and express it as 'I am'. There is something powerful about claiming an identity now before you even feel fully confident that you are that person. The likelihood is that if you say, 'I am an innovative thinker', you probably already are! This exercise helps you see it.
- Expand this exercise and think that if you are an innovative thinker, a thought leader or a motivator, what does that mean in everyday life? How do you behave? What does that mean you do and don't do? What does that mean you stand for and stand against?
- Find facts for this new created identity. Most of us find evidence to back up the negative things we think about ourselves, so try flipping this around and writing down what evidence there is that you *are* this new created identity.
- Get really good at 'arresting' your thoughts. Our brains talk rubbish sometimes, and our emotions are not always reliable. Sometimes our old identities will pull us back and when this happens the voices in our heads start yapping. That is when we need to isolate the destructive thought and 'arrest' it. By that I mean saying to yourself, 'I do not know where that thought has come from. It's not true. You don't have permission to go roaming around my brain like that causing destruction!' Then we metaphorically lock it up. We don't have to act on every thought, but we need get our thoughts under control. Allowing all these thoughts to wander free-range through our minds isn't helpful.
- In 15 years' time, when you look back on this period, what do you want to be true about you? Write it down. Work out what the first step is – do that! Start small and build your confidence. You may want to be a thought leader in the future – it starts with reading a page of a book today!

For your team's created identity:

- Schedule time to talk about these things – what do we all want to be as a team?
- Put to bed some of the things that have been said about you in the past. Maybe you were an 'underachieving department' in the past, but that doesn't mean you have to be that now.
- Be open about what hasn't worked. Identities will have been formed based on what your team have (or haven't) done – own these mistakes and failures. PIXAR reportedly have a 'funeral of ideas' concept where they place the films that aren't going to make it on the altar and talk about what they meant, what they learned from them and how they

will use those lessons going forward. Then they say goodbye. Ending things well is important; we have to find a way of drawing the line and moving on.

- Explore the 'culture canvas' concept, written about in my previous *Time to Think* books – it's a great way to create a new shared identity.

Just because you used to be X, doesn't mean you can't now be Y. I can change and so can you, so let's start that process. If things are holding you back then address them, don't bury them.

Box clever pledge: Identity

My current box is _____ (Date: _____)

I want to be able to be _____ by _____ (date)

I am going to do the following:

1) _____

2) _____

Annotate the quadrant with your own notes. What have you taken away from this chapter?

Future

Programmed identity	Created identity
Reflected identity	Remembered identity

Past

Other — Self

You will find another copy of this quadrant on page 112. Why not put a reminder in your calendar and come back to it in a few months' time and see what has changed?

CHAPTER 7
THE ONE ABOUT TIMING

One of the complexities in our daily jobs (and lives!) is deciding whether to take action or to wait. We can sometimes worry about the right time – whether there ever will be a right time and what will happen if we do something at the wrong time. What we aim for is to make the right decision at the right time. The challenge is that we cannot always know what the 'right' time or decision is; all that we can do is ensure that we engage in detailed thinking so we make the best decision available at the time. We may even need to move away from the concept of 'right' in the first place. Some decisions can be judged 'right' or 'wrong', but so many others cannot. As soon as we use the word 'right' we put enormous pressure on ourselves that can be paralysing. Sometimes we will make the 'right' decision now just to find in six months' time, when the context has changed, that it may have been the 'wrong' one. Perhaps saying, 'I have to make *a* decision' is more freeing?

Some decisions can be made more slowly, and some have to be made quickly. Not all decisions are the same, and therefore we may need different approaches. In his book, *Think Again*, Adam Grant outlines a number of factors that may impact the speed of making a decision. If a decision is irreversible and consequential you will go more slowly than if it reversable and inconsequential, where you may act more quickly. If you are making big decisions but all of them are reversable, you can probably afford to experiment. Consequential decisions need more time. You can use this quadrant as a way of checking yourself, your speed and level of certainty for this decision at this time.

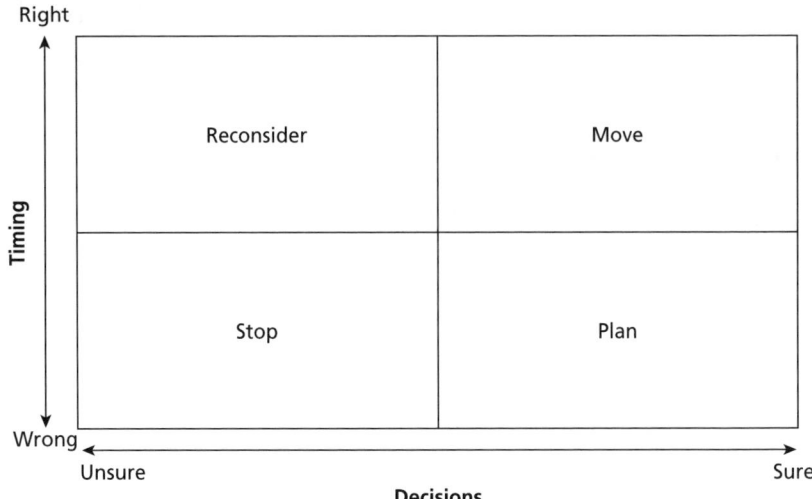

Unpacking the boxes: Where am I now?

When we make any decision, there are some processes we can use to double-check that it's the right one for what we are trying to achieve. You may want to think through these processes individually or even be brave enough to go through them as a team where possible.

Making the right decision

Whenever you are making a decision, it's worth thinking about these steps:

- What is the problem I am trying to resolve?
- Does this decision solve that problem (partially or fully)?
- What are the unintended consequences of this decision?
- Will any of these unintended consequences be so impactful that I should change this decision?
- Have I done a pre-mortem of this decision?
- Who else has contributed to this decision? Is anyone missing?
- Has this decision been debated?
- Have we thought through what this means for different layers of our organisation?
- What do we gain from making this decision?

- Have we checked what the facts say and what our instincts say? Are they aligned?
- Do we have a clear picture of what things will look like once we have made this decision?
- If we have any 'niggles' around this decision, what are they and where are they coming from?

Getting the timing right

Timing is crucial; we can reach the right decision but at the wrong time. It's important to think through the timing of what we are about to do if we have agreed on a decision:

- Why am I doing this now?
- Is this decision time-sensitive?
- If this is urgent, what is at stake?
- What are the risks of moving on this now?
- What are the risks of not moving on this now?
- What makes this the 'right time'?
- Who is it the right time for? The organisation? You? The staff? The metrics?
- If there is fallout, will that impact the timing of anything else?
- Do we have time to implement this well?
- Have people been given the time to work on this?
- What support will people need when we announce our decision?

Once you have answered these questions, look at the quadrant and decide where you are now.

Reconsider

This is the right time but potentially the wrong decision, because you are unsure. It may be the right time because you have capacity, time and support, but the 'rightness' of the timing may be pushing you to make a decision that isn't right. When we get into this box, sometimes it's our impatience that is driving us to a decision at any cost or it's because we just want something resolved. We are more likely to make rushed decisions when we are panicked, bored, frustrated or impatient, and when we have limited time to think and act we want to get on with doing something. Sometimes we want to display a show of power, but in trying to do so we make the wrong decision or make one too quickly. We have to be careful that all of these factors don't lead us to make rash decisions. We can become reckless if we don't stop and reconsider.

Stop

If the timing is wrong and we are unsure about the decision, in most cases we should stop – to do anything else could be a disaster. Sometimes circumstances may mean we have to move forward even though we are not totally sure, but that is usually because we have run out of time to make a more considered decision.

When we agree to stop, we also have to think through this decision:

- What needs to change to make this the right time?
- What needs to change to make this the right decision?
- Why are we not ready now?
- What does stopping look like? Are we stopping the decision but continuing the discussion? Or parking this until another time?
- When are we coming back to review both the timing and the decision?
- Both are wrong at the moment, so which one needs to be right first?

Plan

Right decision, wrong timing. This one is a test of patience. If you are in this box, you really have to analyse what 'right timing' looks like. It's worth asking these questions:

- How did we decide this was the wrong timing?
- What made this 'wrong timing'?
- What would 'right timing' look like?
- What do we need to plan to ensure the next time we decide to act the timing is right?

Move

This position means that, in theory, everything has aligned and you are ready to move forward. You have a 'right' decision and you believe it is the 'right' time. If this is the case, there are some things to consider to ensure the implementation of the decision goes as smoothly as possible:

- What have I communicated about this decision?
- Who needs to know?
- In what order do they need to know?
- How am I communicating the decision?
- How will I ensure people understand the decision?

- Have I carried out a pre-mortem of the fallout, so I can anticipate the unintended consequences of this decision?

Stepping out of the box

Working out what you need to do and what you need to stop (and why) is always a challenge of leadership. Part of coming to any decision is checking our own motivations, emotions and perspectives to ensure we are balanced and wise throughout the process. This is the kind of prompt list that I use to check myself:

1. Have I sought different opinions about this decision?
2. Have I asked people who I suspect will not agree with me?
3. Have I been robustly challenged so I know there are no holes in my plan?
4. Am I responding from a place of 'adult' where I am present and focused?
5. Have I checked my emotional reaction? Am I making this decision because it's safe? Or because I'm frustrated or in a hurry?
6. Have I thought through how I am going to manage the people in this process who will be impacted by this decision?
7. What is the kindest and clearest thing to do in this situation, even if it is hard?
8. What support have I got for when this decision lands and what support do others need?
9. Do I have a clear and compelling (and consistent) narrative as to why I am making this decision?
10. Are there any niggles that I am ignoring? Why am I ignoring it? Deliberately or am I avoiding something I should not ignore?

Not all decisions are significant, and not decisions all have major consequences. However, we owe it to the people we lead to make sure we have examined ourselves, questioned our thoughts and decisions and can demonstrate the courage of our convictions. We must also make sure that our preparation starts during the lead-up to the decision being made or announced. My dad used to say, 'The preparation for a conference happens the night before.' What he meant was that he wanted to be at his best on the day, and so the days before the event he looked after himself. This approach shows respect for ourselves and respect for the people we lead. The same applies to making decisions.

Box clever pledge: Timing

My current box is _____ (Date: _____)

I want to be able to be _____ by _____ (date)

I am going to do the following:

1) _____

2) _____

Annotate the quadrant with your own notes. What have you taken away from this chapter?

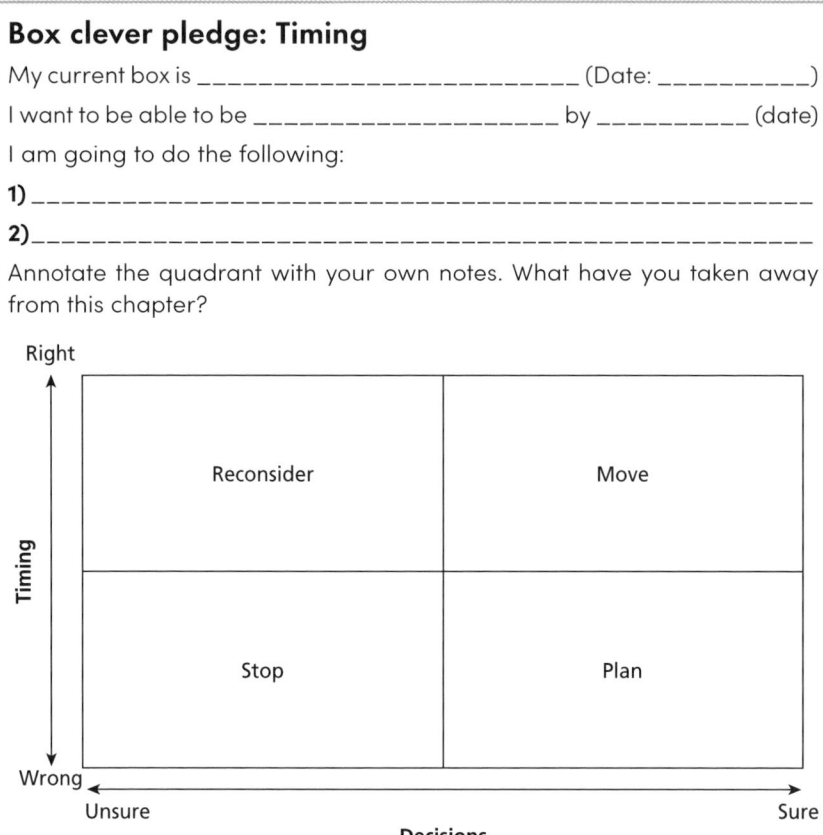

You will find another copy of this quadrant on page 113. Why not put a reminder in your calendar and come back to it in a few months' time and see what has changed?

CHAPTER 8
THE ONE ABOUT PARADOXICAL THINKING

We live in a world that often takes 'either/or' positions. We see this a lot on social media where people tend to go towards one argument or the other and the people who sit somewhere in the middle stay silent. Taking an 'either/or' position can be used as clickbait; it can raise profiles, get you attention and, in some cases, become your 'brand'. What it doesn't do is make you a better thinker or leader or enable you to be open to what you may not be seeing or understanding. When we show no willingness to explore the issues, we may well be missing other opportunities. We certainly miss listening to others who may hold a different view.

The fact of the matter is that two seemingly opposing things can be true at the same time. We can feel more than one feeling in our hearts, have more than one thought in our heads and can reason to the point where we can get comfortable with 'both/and' and not just 'either/or'. It's possible to be both exhausted and energised by your work, excited and anxious about a challenge and to feel delighted for your colleague's promotion while being deeply saddened you didn't get the job. When we face dark and difficult times, whether that be grief, a breakdown of a relationship or another life change, we can feel both sadness for what has happened and relief that something has changed. We are not 'either/or' – to even think that we are diminishes what it is to be human.

If we stay wedded to an 'either/or' mindset we can find ourselves at a disadvantage. The work of Marianne W. Lewis and Wendy K. Smith sheds light on this issue. Their research is summarised in this quadrant, where we see the relationship between how we experience tension and our mindset.

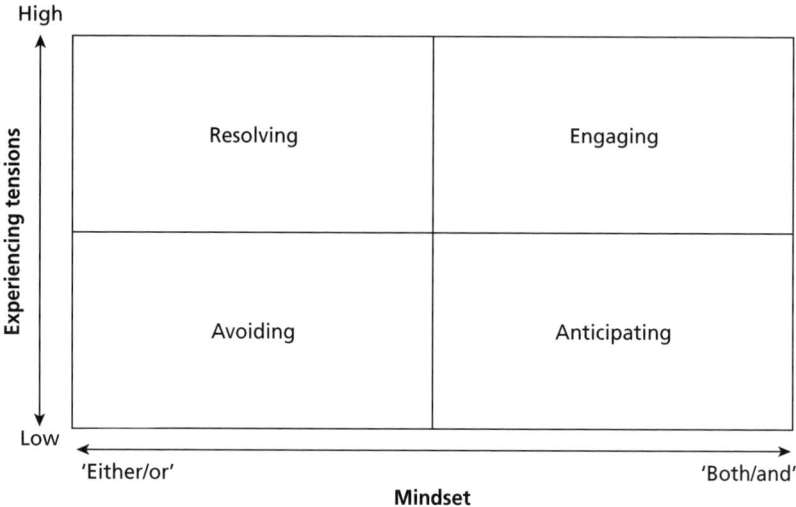

Unpacking the boxes: Where am I now?

At some points in our lives, we can be 'both/and' people. When we acknowledge our emotions and thoughts and spend time unpacking them, we often realise that we are made up of contradictions and are constantly changing. When we feel in control, we can talk about how a work decision could incorporate different ideas into the final decision. The challenge is that the conditions are sometimes not ideal. When tensions are high, time pressure is applied and people are entrenched in their own views it can become a battle where one is 'right' and the other is 'wrong'. Instead of taking this position, how can we move our mindset to be more 'both/and' and less either/or?

What prevents us from being able to think in 'both/and' more often? In their book, *Both/And Thinking*, Wendy K. Smith and Marianne K. Lewis explore some of the challenges around tensions and how we can embrace them. They argue there are three core topics that have been a crucial part of understanding their research: tensions, dilemmas and paradoxes.

Tensions

These are situations where expectations and demands are in opposition; we can feel pulled in different directions. Tension is an overarching theme for dilemmas and paradoxes, but they are neither good nor bad. The right kind of tension can drive creativity and innovation, but the wrong type can lead to defensiveness and destruction. The impact of tension depends on how we respond to them – we can feel uncomfortable and anxious and forced to make a choice.

Dilemmas

This is where we could go one way or another and feel the pressure to choose between different options. We weigh up the advantages and disadvantages and then find ourselves stuck. We try to think ourselves into a position that will bring a good and lasting decision, but often we can't find a solution and we can't move forward. When we get stuck going back and forth in our arguments, we can find ourselves in a vicious cycle of negative thinking.

Paradoxes

Smith and Lewis define paradoxes as 'interdependent, persistent contradictions that lurk within our present dilemmas.' These can often seem ridiculous because they integrate contradictions that can both be true, even though they are opposite. We can want change because we want to feel excited and energised, and at the same time want stability because we want to feel grounded and secure. They are not oppositional – they are interlinked. 'What do I want?' is the question we have to answer when we feel two different things at the same time, and we have to explore how these two opposing ideas link.

How we experience these tensions, dilemmas and paradoxes (and our attitude towards them) is what creates the quadrant we are exploring. Sometimes we think we know which box we are in, but Smith and Lewis have designed an inventory that helps plot where you are actually sitting. This position is not forever; it's where you may be now, but change can happen.

There are two sections of the inventory: the first section covers how you experience tensions, and the second covers the mindset you adopt as you engage with these tensions. The version below is a shorter version of the inventory. If you are interested in doing a fuller version to generate your score so you can plot it on a graph more mathematically, then head to paradox.lerner.udel.edu, where you can take the inventory and receive helpful feedback on where you currently sit. You may also want to share this with your colleagues and have them complete it to see what the balance in your team is like.

BOX CLEVER

Read each of these 16 statements and use the following scale:

1 – Strongly disagree
2 – Disagree
3 – Slightly disagree
4 – Neither agree nor disagree
5 – Slightly agree
6 – Agree
7 – Strongly agree

Paradox mindset inventory	Strongly disagree	Disagree	Slightly disagree	Neither agree nor disagree	Slightly agree	Agree	Strongly agree
Experiencing tensions							
1. I sometimes hold in my mind two ideas that seem contradictory when they appear together	1	2	3	4	5	6	7
2. I often have competing demands that need to be addressed at the same time	1	2	3	4	5	6	7
3. I often have goals that contradict each other	1	2	3	4	5	6	7
4. I often have to meet contradictory requirements	1	2	3	4	5	6	7
5. My work is filled with tensions and contradictions	1	2	3	4	5	6	7
6. I often need to decide between opposing alternatives	1	2	3	4	5	6	7
7. When I examine a problem, the possible solutions usually seem contradictory	1	2	3	4	5	6	7

CHAPTER 8 THE ONE ABOUT PARADOXICAL THINKING

Paradox mindset inventory	Strongly disagree	Disagree	Slightly disagree	Neither agree nor disagree	Slightly agree	Agree	Strongly agree
Paradox mindset							
8. When I consider conflicting perspectives, I gain a better understanding of an issue	1	2	3	4	5	6	7
9. I am comfortable dealing with conflicting demands at the same time	1	2	3	4	5	6	7
10. Accepting contradictions is essential for my success	1	2	3	4	5	6	7
11. Tension between ideas energises me	1	2	3	4	5	6	7
12. I enjoy it when I manage to pursue contradictory goals	1	2	3	4	5	6	7
13. I often experience myself as simultaneously embracing conflicting demands	1	2	3	4	5	6	7
14. I am comfortable working on tasks that contradict each other	1	2	3	4	5	6	7
15. I feel uplifted when I realise two opposites can be true.	1	2	3	4	5	6	7
16. I feel energised when I manage to address contradictory issue	1	2	3	4	5	6	7

For your 'experiencing tensions' score, average all your answers from statements 1 to 7 (the average score for a white-collar professional is 4.38). For your 'paradox mindset' score, average all your answers from questions 8 to 16 (the average score for a white-collar professional is 4.9). You can now plot these scores on the quadrant to see which box you fall into.

Resolving zone

In the 'resolving zone', you experience a high level of tension and want a decision to be made and dilemmas to be resolved (preferably at speed). You may find:

- You are focused on the pros and cons in a situation and deciding on the right option in a specific situation.
- You can see the tensions but generally you want to come to a conclusive response.
- You can move a decision forward, but because you have focused on a single choice you may have limited other options and more creative and innovative thinking.
- That tensions often resurface when they are resolved quickly and so this isn't a long-term solution, rather kicking the can down the road.

There are more creative and long-term solutions to be found if we can see the opportunities in opposing views as we engage with them. Giving ourselves time to think through decisions will help here. There are ways we can encourage people to come out of this zone:

- Provide pre-reading that outlines all dilemmas.
- Encourage messy conversation and discussion that is deliberately *not* resulting in an action or decision.
- Try to reduce the high level of tension by being clear about what is required in this decision. If you are the leader, be clear with people that you want their broad 'both/and' thinking more than you want a decision. If you struggle with this, tell people you want to see all the thinking before making a decision and ask questions that help you explore the issues. Prepare thought leadership pieces, not just proposals with the answers.
- In your language, avoid 'either/or'. Instead, ask 'What would having both look like?' or 'How can we achieve X at the same time as ensuring Y?' It will feel messier, but this is where better thinking happens.

Avoiding zone

In the 'avoiding zone', there is low tension but an 'either/or' mindset. If your score places you in here, then the following may describe your approach:

- You both want to avoid tensions and get them resolved (or you may only be exposed to limited tension).
- Under pressure, you may approach dilemmas as issues that need to be solved rather than opportunities to be explored. This position can lead to reduced performance, innovation and satisfaction.
- If the tension increases you may find yourself even more firmly in this box or moving to the 'resolving zone', where under increasing pressure you just want it done and off the list.

If you can seek out more tension but reframe them as opportunities to stretch your thinking, you may become more innovative and creative, having thoughts you have previously not allowed yourself to have.

To pull us out of this place, we may need to:

- Spend more time in action-free meetings and dedicate time to discussion.
- Deliberately take a different view and try to think that line of enquiry through.
- Look at case studies of other teams and organisations who face the same dilemmas and discuss the merits of them as well as the challenges.
- Bring other people into meetings so you can see more, think differently and get uncomfortable – this is what moves us out of the avoiding zone.

Anticipating zone

The 'anticipating zone' is where we have less tension and are perhaps more likely to practice 'both/and' thinking. In this zone, the following may be true:

- You are ready to think 'both/and' but the tension is low (or you are unaware of it).
- Tension can rise quickly, and you may find that when that happens you become aware of conflicts that you had not been aware of previously or had ignored or just hadn't seen clearly.
- As the tension rises, you may find yourself able to be more creative and innovative. In this position you may want to actively try and seek out tension and deliberately find ideas that are juxtapositions because it breeds new thinking.

In any meeting, you have a job to do! You can help bring about new thinking, try to move people away from the polarity of their thinking and move people towards 'both/and'.

Engaging zone

If you place yourself in the 'engaging zone', you tend to experience more tension and accept and feel comfortable with the paradoxes than underpin the dilemmas you face. That means that you:

- Recognise that paradoxes are 'contradictory, interdependent and persistent' (Lewis and Smith, 2022).
- Appreciate that paradoxes can never be fully resolved but you can engage with them in a productive way.

- Can take seemingly opposing ideas and value how they can be linked, reinforce one another or make you think differently.
- Accept the challenge of the uncertain (and sometimes scary) nature of sitting here, because clear cut answers don't simply appear. Here you are comfortable with the mess and are capable (and willing) to think around the issues.

Lewis and Smith's research shows that people who place themselves here and adopt 'both/and' thinking perform better and are the most innovative and satisfied with their work.

Some things to consider here if this is you:

- You may be here but it's unlikely that all of your team are, so how are you going to ensure you are not dragged into making quick decisions? How can you enable your team to be comfortable with the discomfort of (what may look like) getting nowhere fast?
- How will you ensure that you stay in this place and are not hurried into making a decision that has become 'either/or'?
- How will you look after yourself so you keep your ability to deal with high tension and your 'both/and' mindset? When does this slip for you? When you are tired? In a rush? Overworking? Under pressure from others?

Stepping out of the box

We can change our mindset about whatever situation we may find ourselves in, but if we are going to step outside of the box we are in, we need to be aware of where we may find ourselves. We need to be aware of how we think, what we feel and how we act – these three things can make us better or make us worse, but it depends on how we do them. If we find ourselves in patterns that do not serve us well, we become stuck in a vicious cycle. Part of moving into the 'engaging zone' is breaking habits that are restricting us.

In 1976, psychologist Aaron Beck talked about the theory of cognitive distortions, which was popularised by David Burns in the 1980s when he created some common names to exemplify the theory. 'Thinking traps', as they are now known, ramp up the tension and can send us down rabbit holes. They move us to a black and white position, which means we are the opposite to 'both/and' – this level of polarisation often does not serve us (or our colleagues or loved ones) well. We can also start over-compensating if we get stuck in a thinking trap – 'If you say this, I will go to the opposite extreme and say that.'

None of these approaches are going to work if we want to spend more time in the engaging zone. Cognitive distortions are the ways our mind convinces us that one thing is true when in reality it's not. When we get into negative and polarised thinking patterns, we don't think well and don't feel great. We become negative because our mindset has become negative. The good news is that we can change our behaviours by noticing them and catching them as we see them cropping up.

If we want to be in the engaging zone, there are thinking traps that we need to avoid. There are many traps out there, but these are the ones that I think are most prevalent.

- **Mind reading.** This is when we assume we know what other people are thinking even though often nothing has been said. We also usually assume the worst and then react to that feeling. We emotionally leak what we are feeling, other people respond and then it becomes a self-fulfilling prophecy when we then think we were right all along.
- **Fortune-telling.** This is when we predict things will turn out badly and start speaking negatively about something that hasn't even happened yet. For example, 'This is never going to work, I just know this is going to end badly.'
- **Black and white thinking.** When we are too 'and/or' rather than 'both/and'. We lose the nuance and often lose compassion, empathy and understanding at the same time. It becomes a battle of right versus wrong and good versus bad, all of which can turn you into a human wrecking ball.
- **Filtering.** When we filter, we only pay attention to negative aspects rather than positive ones. This stops us thinking about other possibilities.
- **Catastrophising.** This involves imagining the worst possible thing that could happen. Used in a pre-mortem context this can be helpful, as stepping into that thinking for a time can ensure that you make good decisions, and it opens up other discussions and options. However, when we magnify situations, we exaggerate and make sweeping statements. We can also catastrophise and minimise ourselves (or the situation) by saying things like, 'I don't need to think differently because I'm nowhere near as good as everyone else who can do that, and I will be exposed.'
- **Over-generalisation.** This can stop us seeing nuance. We can start with a position and then make sweeping statements about much bigger things and that can force us into 'and/or' thinking, which isn't helpful.

- **Labelling.** Labelling is when we say 'you are' or 'I am' rather than 'I have noticed that I have feelings of...'. Labelling people is rarely helpful, especially if we are trying to engage in paradoxical thinking. We are not just this or that – we are complex!
- **Personalisation.** This is where we think everything someone does or says is a personal attack. When we are here, we get defensive and negative. We must be able to see behind behaviours and see alternative interpretations if we are ever going to become 'both/and' thinkers.
- **'Should' statements.** We sometimes make rules about what should and shouldn't happen. Although this may look helpful, it isn't if we are trying to be innovative and find new solutions.
- **Emotional reasoning.** Here, we take our emotions as evidence of the truth. 'I feel right, so I am right' is problematic in many situations. If we use our emotions as facts, we can end up in cycles of negative thinking and be totally closed off to alternative interpretations. We usually have emotional reactions to situations, but we need to be careful not to jump to dangerous conclusions on the back of them.

If we want to spend more time in the engaging zone, then we can. We can change and adapt. However, in order to do so we must think differently and ask questions that will move us away from polarisation. Here are some questions that I have used that can get us in a better position to be able to think in 'both/and':

1. What are 10 paradoxes that we want to navigate in this organisation? For example, 'We want people to be loyal and feel they belong to us *and* to encourage people to grow and leave for other opportunities.'
2. If we were to set up an organisation that would compete against ours, what would we create?
3. If there were no rules and we could start again, what information would we want to know before we started?
4. How can we make A and B true so we can accommodate both?
5. What are the multiple truths in this dilemma we face?

As Maya Angelou (2009) said, 'If you cannot make a change, change the way you have been thinking. You might find a new solution.'

CHAPTER 8 THE ONE ABOUT PARADOXICAL THINKING

Box clever pledge: Paradoxical thinking

My current box is _____ (Date: _____)

I want to be able to be _____ by _____ (date)

I am going to do the following:

1) _____

2) _____

Annotate the quadrant with your own notes. What have you taken away from this chapter?

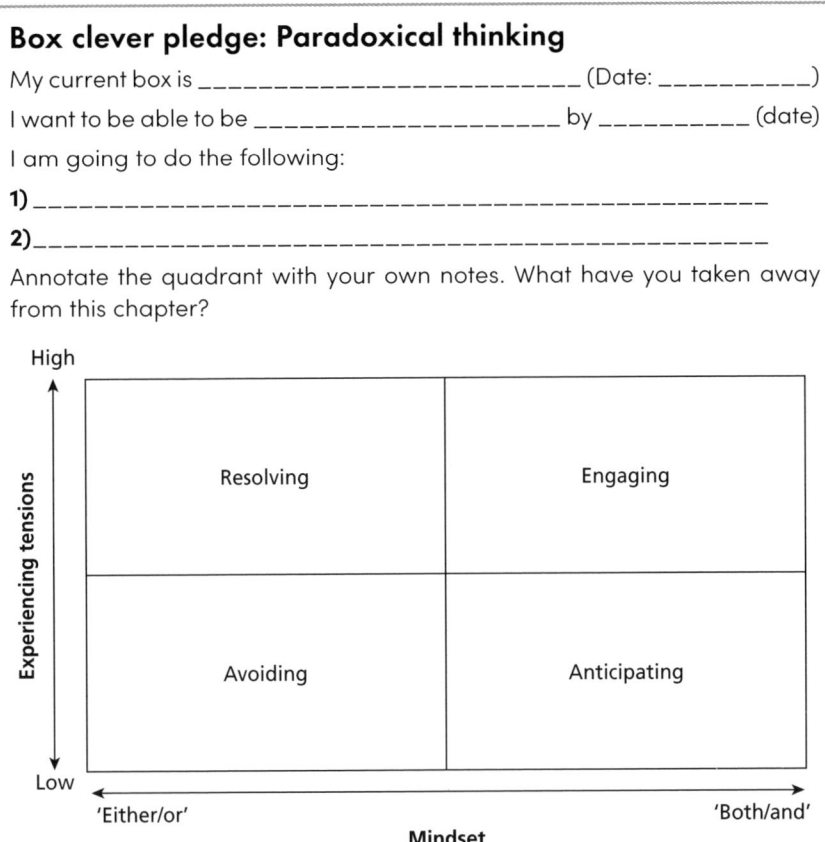

You will find another copy of this quadrant on page 114. Why not put a reminder in your calendar and come back to it in a few months' time and see what has changed?

CHAPTER 9
THE ONE ABOUT ISSUES OVER TIME

We have explored the issue of paradoxical thinking and the timing and confidence of decisions, but this quadrant (although linked to those issues) helps us see things from a different angle. Designed by Nitin Nohria, a former dean of Harvard Business School, this quadrant helps us identify where we need to respond and why.

In a 2018 survey that explored where CEOs spent their time, the results found that on average they spent 36% of their time in reactive mode (the highest score was 81% and the lowest was 14%). The questions this quadrant helps us ask (and answer) are:

- Where should we be spending our time and on what?
- How does any leader know where they should be placing their attention?
- How do we get the balance between being reactive and being proactive?
- How can we make a calculation of the issue that presents itself *and* the significance of this issue?

You may be familiar with the Eisenhower Matrix (see chapter 11, page 93), which categorises issues by their urgency and importance, but Nohria's quadrant is different. This 'reactive management framework' quadrant considers how events may evolve so we can be more discerning over what gets our time and what doesn't.

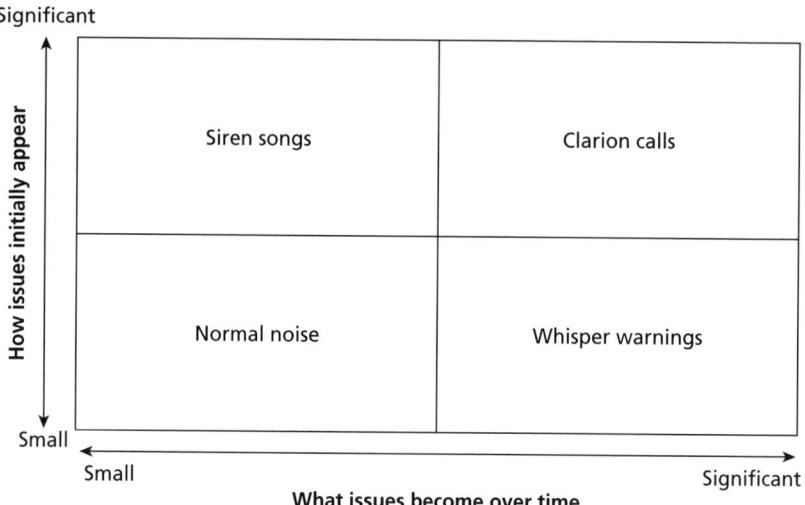

Unpacking the boxes: Where am I now?

Nohria argues that to get better at responding effectively to unfolding events, leaders need to become better at assessing the significance of the issue and how it may increase or decrease over time. These two things plotted against each other give us the following four ways of assessing the situation so we can deploy our time appropriately.

Siren songs: Watch and wait

If something is a 'siren song', then we think the issue is significant when in fact it's small (at the moment). This is where we need discernment; in this area, we have to watch and wait and not overact. The whole concept of a siren song is a reference to the appeal of something that is alluring but also potentially harmful or dangerous. In mythology, the sirens sang to passing sailors to tempt them into dangerous territory where they would be shipwrecked. Many a leader has heard a call and been dragged into something that has been deceptive, destructive, damaging and dangerous. When these issues come along, they come with a real sense of urgency. We are tempted to clear the diary and stop everything to respond. There are some risks involved, which is why we have to be wise:

- Sometimes paying too much attention to these siren songs gives more energy to the problem and makes it worse. We can create more of a controversy than there needed to be.

- We can respond out of sheer panic – the media have phoned, someone has threatened something, a product hasn't worked, there's been a complaint. If we wait (or even sleep on it), we can see whether this really does need our attention.
- Siren songs take all our attention away from other things that may be more significant. When we are distracted, we may be neglecting something that really did need our time and attention when we failed to give it any.

The best advice when you are hearing the 'calls of the siren' is to:

- Wait and perhaps sleep on it.
- Keep calm and composed while you wait.
- Beware of the thinking traps we discussed in chapter 8 (see page 63).
- Seek out the facts and see what information comes in.
- Stay informed with the people on the front line.
- See if things calm down.

There are many examples in recent history where there have been 'siren songs' on social media and newspaper headlines have been written, just to discover within a couple of days that it's all disappeared and amounted to nothing. If leaders had jumped in too soon, then they would have fuelled the fire and kept it going longer. The job of a leader is to discern when we need to respond and when we need to stay quiet.

Normal noise: Don't get drawn in

If the issue appears small, it may well remain small over time. There is always something going on in every organisation; we experience small ripples, but if it's not likely to build into a wave (or a tsunami) then it probably doesn't need your attention. There may be issues with complaints, something that has been overlooked, a mistake that needs to be rectified, deadlines that have been missed or some organisational wins or losses, but if these issues are part of the everyday and you have teams (and procedures) to manage them, they probably don't need your time or energy. As the leader, if you are involving yourself in minor things that someone else could (and should) be handling, you will get drawn in.

The desire to get drawn in can be strong. Many of us like rescuing or jumping into the detail to 'fix' something because it helps us feel useful, perhaps even heroic! However, we mustn't get drawn in and distracted by the noise. That doesn't mean to say we show no interest though. Our role if we believe that the problem is small is to:

- Resist the temptation to jump in.
- Trust your teams but check that things are happening as you would expect them to.
- Check that what you think you know is the truth. 'Verifying' what you have been told can involve staff surveys, customer questionnaires and 'init' interviews (the opposite of 'exit' interviews), where we ask staff while they are *in* our organisation how they are finding things.
- Pulse surveys that go deeper into the issue you want to check.
- Check in with leaders as to whether the small issue has been resolved and ask them how they know.

If the issue is small and has stayed small (or been resolved), we don't need to give it any further attention. Sometimes these issues grow, and so while we are not getting drawn in we still need to keep an eye on how they are being managed.

Whisper warnings: Nip things in the bud

'Whisper warnings' are sometimes hard to discern from the first two categories we have unpacked so far. These are some characteristics of problems that are whisper warnings:

- They appear minor but have the potential to grow into something more major.
- If these things grow, they could present a threat to you or the organisation, ranging from reputational damage to financial ruin.
- They may appear to be insignificant, which means they can stay hidden – perhaps a little whisper here or there.
- There is a risk that as they are only whispers no one has said anything explicit, but there is a whiff of something that isn't right.
- People may be making excuses that seem viable but cover something darker, such as, 'We know they're a little assertive and rude but you know what they're like.' There may not be a formal complaint (yet) or an accusation (yet), but this is the whisper you need to catch before it becomes a shout.
- Whispers often happen in a number of places that look unconnected. It is our job as leaders to start connecting the dots, look for patterns and work out what is actually happening.

CHAPTER 9 THE ONE ABOUT ISSUES OVER TIME

- It may present as discontent within the team, so don't ignore this. Stay open and curious rather than dismissing it.
- We may have been hearing whispers for weeks, months or even years and no one has acted. Eventually these issues will be voiced – do not ignore these things. Many organisations would tell you the cost (emotionally, financially, reputationally) of having a scandal that could (and should) have been addressed earlier.

Not every whisper warning will need your undivided attention. The challenging thing as a leader is that we need to determine what has the potential to get bigger and what doesn't. If we get this wrong and we ignore the whispers, the damage that can be unleashed won't be repaired easily.

Here's how we can be in the best position to spot whisper warnings:

- We can pull the 'Andon Cord'. This is a physical or digital cord that signals a problem in manufacturing and can stop production, so the issue is addressed. This may mean withdrawing a letter, policy or product and investigating immediately.
- We can make a decision with a member of staff.
- We can arrange to speak to someone who is upset.
- We can put together a response before the news breaks.
- We can phone the media and ask for a conversation to manage the fall out and explain what is at risk (especially if there are children or vulnerable people involved in the story).
- We can ensure internal communications are clear and forward thinking.
- We can put together contingency plans to address potential escalation.
- We can show humanity and apologise if there is an error and explain how we are going to sort out whatever has gone wrong.
- Before there are any whispers, we can plan what we would do in such a situation. Speed is sometimes of the essence, so planning in advance (based on principles) can save valuable time and reduce stress.

We know that leaders who respond early are more likely to bring a situation under control.

Clarion calls: Be all in

These situations are potentially less challenging than the other three simply because they are easier to see. You are not having to work out what category these situations are in – they are very visible! And if something has become a 'clarion call', the issue is likely to be significant. The only response to this situation is to be 'all in'.

There are many situations that could fit into examples of 'clarion calls', such as product failure, financial irregularity, fraud, a condemning report, sexual harassment claims, corruption, crises or a deadly accident. We hope that we never have to face these things, but unfortunately they may occur. We must be prepared to act quickly but not rashly.

These situations will be highly visible, and because of this it's much easier to mobilise your organisation into action. Limits that existed before (budget or guidelines, for example) may all be lifted now that a crisis has hit, giving you more freedom to match resource to the crisis.

When we hear a 'clarion call', we have to:

- Dedicate time, energy and thinking to the situation. Be 'all in'.
- Shift our (and the leadership team's) priorities to the main incident.
- Get personally involved – this is all hands on deck for all the leadership.
- Avoid the temptation to go inwards and handle it all ourselves.
- Reach out to obtain information, ideas and resource from others.
- Be aware that while other departments will have their own agendas (which is their job!) you must keep a grasp of the whole to lead the organisation forward. HR will view things differently to Finance, who will see it differently to the data teams. These departments need to tell us what they can see, but we need to see it all.
- Show empathy and compassion towards the people who are impacted by what has happened. Whatever has happened will be causing anxiety, stress, fear and perhaps even embarrassment or shame. We must try and understand (and anticipate) how people will be affected.
- We must do all of the above while focusing on doing what is right instead of feeling pressured to do what may be 'safe'. We must take risks, be brave and be led by what we (and our organisation) believe to be right.

Stepping out of the box

Nohria suggests three approaches that can be used by leaders so they can react effectively to the unfolding events they may face. His three-step process involves sensing, sizing and responding.

Sensing

We need to ensure that the systems we have around us don't block out the signals that we need to sense. For example, if someone organises your diary, you may not always get a sense of who is asking for time, or why. People may be asking to meet about something that doesn't appear urgent or significant to anyone else, but it may turn out to be. Someone else may be reading emails, which means you may not be able to sense what is coming in that needs your attention (even if it appears to be minor). These processes can be helpful in streamlining work for a leader so they can stay focused on their priorities, but sometimes important 'tells' pop up in these processes.

We can do the following in order to sense when things need our attention:

- Be mindful and present in meetings so you are more likely to spot the subtle signs that may indicate a concern. The chat in the room before it starts, as well as the body language, can both be indicators.
- Keep asking people for feedback, check out your assumptions and test them.
- Ensure that people are in the best position to tell you the truth. Ask them to feed back on something specific (that you are already sensing) to determine if they have seen any evidence.
- Commit to ensuring your workplace has psychological safety. If it doesn't, events may go from small to big quickly without your awareness.
- Engage in 'sensemaking', a term coined by organisational theorist Karl Weick. This is when we recognise patterns, perspectives and data, and we start to look at them together to make meaning clear. When we do this, it helps us mentally process complex situations that can feel ambiguous. We get better (and faster!) at this the longer we have been doing it.

Sizing

Sizing a situation up requires skills in predicting and forecasting, as well as pattern recognition. For example, we have to size up the situation so we know the difference between whisper warnings and siren songs. To give ourselves the best chance of being able to 'size' well, we need to:

- Use our emotional intelligence to gauge the significance of the issue.
- Use our knowledge of our people to size something up – we know the people who are good indicators for something not being right.

- Use our contextual intelligence of external factors to help make predictions.
- Recognise that different teams will see things with different degrees of urgency depending on how it impacts them. Some may place too much weight to an incident or overreact, so we need to size up everything we are being told and then decide what to do.
- As leaders, we are the ones who must have a sense of proportion and perspective. We are the ones who need to distinguish the insignificant from the important, understand the wider picture and potential consequences and join the dots in order to make an assessment of how we move forward. It is our own judgement that has to be acted on (even if we delegate and involve others), so we need to believe in the decision we are making.

Responding

To respond well, we need to size and sense but we also need to decide what to do. One of the challenges here is that we need an adaptive response. Although sensing and sizing can happen while we are on the 'balcony' looking at events, action must happen on the dancefloor. Leaders shift between the two perspectives, rather like chess players. We have the strategy in mind and can see the overall game, but we still have to move the pieces on the board in a specific order and time.

There are approaches that can aid us in our response:

- Keep deliberately flicking between balcony and dancefloor. See the big picture, go and make a change and get back to the balcony to see the impact – and repeat!
- Don't commit yourself to a fixed trajectory at the start; if the facts change, so will you. Unexpected events happen and things change, so make sure to be flexible and agile so you can adapt as you need to.

It's hard to calculate what is a big problem in the making and what sounds big but will not result in anything significant. Nohria's 'reactive management framework' gives us a way into important conversations and a common language that helps us align our response.

CHAPTER 9 THE ONE ABOUT ISSUES OVER TIME

Box clever pledge: Issues over time

My current box is _____ (Date: _____)

I want to be able to be _____ by _____ (date)

I am going to do the following:

1) _____

2) _____

Annotate the quadrant with your own notes. What have you taken away from this chapter?

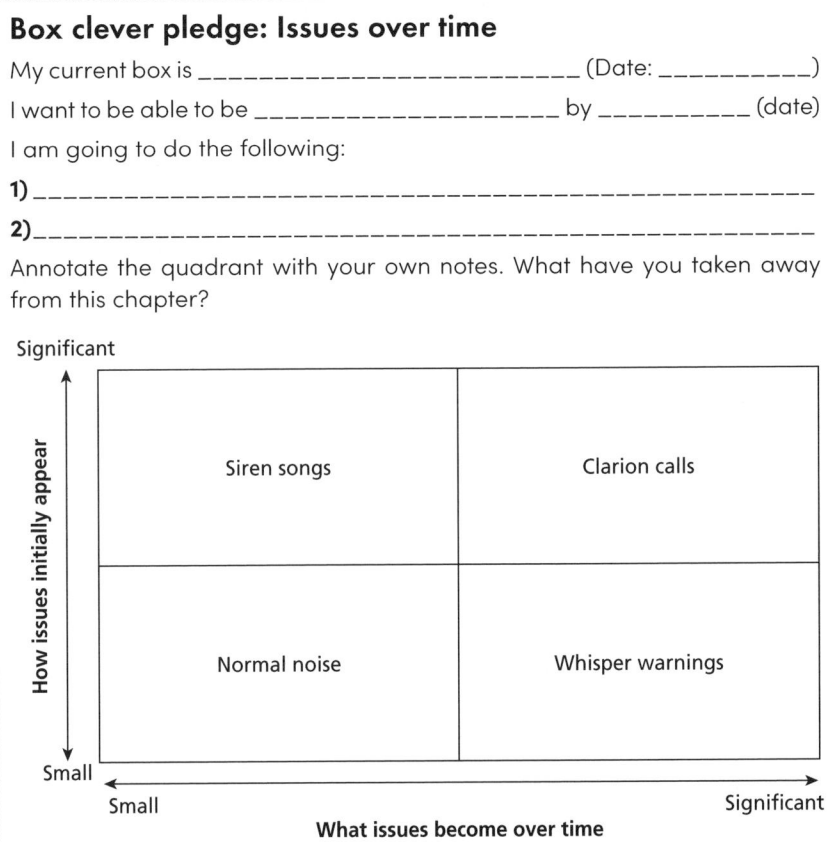

You will find another copy of this quadrant on page 115. Why not put a reminder in your calendar and come back to it in a few months' time and see what has changed?

CHAPTER 10
THE ONE ABOUT OUR ENERGY

We are coming to the end of *Box Clever*, and we've looked at a lot of quadrants together. You will (I hope) have identified what needs to change and how you may drive that change. What you may not have identified is who will help you on the road to change.

People need people. Connection and belonging are such powerful feelings when we experience them. We were made for connection, yet our world is facing an epidemic of loneliness (WHO, 2023). People seem on so many levels more connected through technology but are less so in reality. If we suffer from loneliness, it may be harder to connect, therefore it is harder to trust. When it is harder to trust it is easier to be cynical and lack hope.

In his excellent book, *The Laws of Connection*, David Robson outlines 13 rules. These are things that help us feel like we are connected, we can trust, we can have hope, and we are seen and can see others.

1. Be consistent in your treatment of others.
2. Create a mutual understanding.
3. Trust that others like you as much as you like them.
4. Check your assumptions.
5. Demonstrate active attention and engage in self-disclosure.
6. Praise people generously and specifically.
7. Be open about your vulnerabilities and value honesty over kindness – but practice both!
8. Do not fear envy. Enjoy 'confelicity' which means to take joy in others success – the opposite of schadenfreude!
9. Ask for help when you need it, knowing that it creates bonds.
10. Offer emotional support to those who need it, but don't force it on them.
11. Be civil and curious in disagreements, and show interest in the other side's views.

12. Choose forgiveness over spite; look at the big picture in arguments.
13. Reach out to those people who are missing in your life and let them know they are still part of your thoughts.

Perhaps you are wondering what these rules have to do with you and your leadership. Well, I would argue everything. We know from the surveys that have appeared in this book so far on optimism, flourishing and handling tension that the people who we work with *do* make a difference to us and the way we work. As leaders, our time is spent working with a vast number of people, and we pour ourselves out but sometimes feel exhausted or even drained as a result.

In my 20s, I was a people pleaser (not that I knew that then – I thought I was just being 'good' or 'kind') and I invested my time in whoever demanded it. Sometimes this was with people who left me feeling positive and energised, but often I didn't feel like that; however lovely or well-meaning the people, I left them feeling utterly exhausted. I wanted to be helpful, to serve others and to work with people who needed my time, but I recognised that somewhere along the line my balance had been lost. It was at the point when I was feeling like I was beyond my capacity (and so, so tired), that someone recommended I read a book called *Restoring Your Spiritual Passion* by Gordan McDonald.

The book, aimed originally at people who are in faith-based ministry, unpacked the idea of burnout. McDonald suggests that although all the people may need our time, we should not spend our time with all the people equally. The reason we are exhausted and lacking in passion is because we haven't paid enough attention to where our attention is going. In short, in our desire to give of ourselves, we have found ourselves emotionally overdrawn – giving so much out and getting not enough back. I felt like a light was switched on, and once I saw what was happening, I couldn't unsee it. The quadrant we are about to explore is inspired by McDonald's work.

Unpacking the boxes: Where are you now?

Before we jump into this quadrant, it is worth giving some disclaimers. I love people. I will spend time with those who need it and want to serve others, and those things have never changed about me. But if I want to be at my best, I have to work out where my energy goes and how I can have deposits coming into the emotional bank account as well as debits going out. I don't have enough energy to go around all the people who want it, and neither do you. The deposits and the debits in themselves are not the problem – managing our energy levels is. Rather like actual bank accounts, our *emotional* accounts need balancing.

The challenge is when we have too much energy going out and not enough energy coming back in. We must work with all the people in our care, but we should also pay attention to what this is doing to us to make sure we can get the right balance. We need to ensure our time is not all placed in one area or another but that the balance is working for us. There is no right place to be in this quadrant; we should be spread across all four boxes. This is an exercise of balance between the boxes, and it may change daily or weekly.

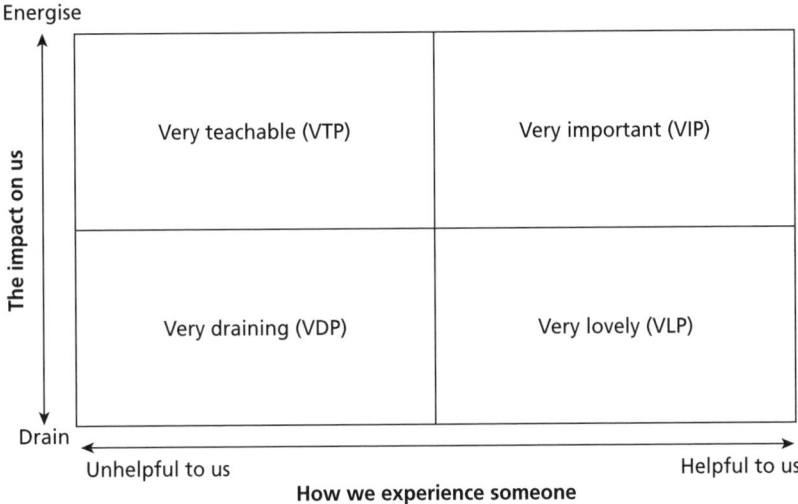

Before we start unpacking, these labels are not meant for individual people – they are meant to describe how we are feeling and the impact on our energy levels. This is about how we experience people. A group of people I find inspiring, you may find draining – that is okay. It isn't about the person; it's about our reaction *to* them and what happens to our energy levels.

Very teachable

These are the people in your life who energise you because they are teachable; they want to learn and can be taught. They may not be helpful to you now, but they will become helpful the more they learn and grow. They can buy into our vision, follow direction and learn to lead. Although they take a lot of investment at the start (they can't be helpful immediately), they will be part of succession planning. We have to be patient with people who are teachable, sometimes slowing down to explain things to them so they understand. These people should exist in every organisation, and we should be committed to growing them and allocating time with them.

Very draining

This is the box we need to be aware of because of what happens to us. Sometimes, for whatever reason, we feel drained by people. Perhaps this happens in challenging circumstances and we find it hard to cope, so we are on edge. Or maybe they take from us, and we don't feel like anything will ever be enough, or nothing changes, so we get frustrated.

It's likely that it takes a lot of investment from us to manage this situation. People who are draining are probably unaware of their effect on our energy levels, but our job is to be aware that if we spend too much of our time with people who drain our energy, then that energy is going to be spent more quickly. Our enthusiasm and passion may wane, as well as our ideas. This doesn't mean we shouldn't spend time with them (we should at times), and it doesn't mean it's their fault (we can't be energised by *everyone*). It isn't something we can necessarily fix, but we shouldn't always avoid people who make us feel like this. We can help and support – we just need to be mindful of how many people we can give our support to.

Great leadership means we can interact and lead all kinds of different personalities. But if we spend the majority of our time with people who we find draining, we won't find the energy, connection and joy that we need and we will find things harder. To stay balanced and in control of ourselves, we need to ensure we have some time with people who can re-energise us. A reminder at this point too: for someone else, *you* may be the very draining person. Let's not make the mistake of assuming that we are not draining!

People you find draining will take your time, not just your energy, and this is time that may be better used elsewhere. Although we should give the time, we should not give up our whole calendars.

Very lovely

Most people in our lives are in this area; they are lovely, likeable people. We can enjoy spending time with them; it can be pleasant, they are often helpful, but we are not energised while we are with them or when we have left them. If we are struggling with something and we want someone to challenge us, understand us and help us get our mojo back, it probably isn't the people in this box we turn to. Yet we need them, rely on them and will be grateful for them.

We can spend lots of time with people who are lovely and find it encouraging to be in their presence. It is unlikely that we would go to them in a crisis or to be energised or inspired, not because they aren't lovely, but because they don't provide those things to us. This isn't about them; it's about what we need and who and what we connect with.

The lovely people may enjoy spending time with us; they may build our egos, and may be loyal and faithful. They can be wonderful people. They don't, however, build our passion and energy. It's sometimes hard to put some boundaries in place with people like this who are genuinely great people. The majority of people we work with will be in this box – we couldn't do life or work without them.

Very important

These are the people who are both helpful and energise you. This is the winning combination, and we all need a few people who are in this group. There will be fewer people in here than in the other boxes. These people ignite our passion, share our workload and let us share our burdens and our emotions (however complex or messy). It's not perfect, but we know we are better together than we would be separately – and that is known by both of us.

We help each other perform better, be better and lead better, and we help each other to chase the right things. We celebrate each other's successes and are there in the disappointments. You may have things in common with these people, even if you may be very different. They will challenge you, but they care. They will speak the truth in love. They will be quick to listen and slow to speak. If you have people like this in your life, you will not feel as alone and are likely to feel both braver and safer.

The sad thing is that we often don't make as much time for these people because we feel we ought to spend time with the other groups. Spending time with these people will bring significantly more benefit to you and your leadership. These people enable you to be at your best so you can serve others better. These people are often colleagues or friends – or both. They are important because of the impact they have on you. They are also very precious, so make time for them. Everyone benefits when you do.

Stepping out of the box

This quadrant doesn't require you to move boxes or take just one position – this one is about balancing the boxes. We can't have all the people we interact with in just one of the boxes, as there needs to be an even spread.

Where our energy goes and how we get re-energised is a crucial part of managing (and balancing) our own leadership. Try to think about the following:

- Looking across all four boxes, where are you short? Where do you have an imbalance?
- Who are the people who are important to you and re-energise you? How many of them are there?
- When you are interacting with these VIPs in your life, what are the benefits to you?
- Now look at your diary – how much time do you spend with your VIPs? What prevents you from engaging with them more?
- Who are the people who are teachable and trainable at work?
- What do you do to invest in them so that they can be more effective? How could you enable them to thrive and be even more helpful to you and your organisation?
- How many people are in the 'draining' category? Have you identified why you find being with them draining? It is important to know this because sometimes you can put things in place to reduce the impact, for example limiting time with them, being with a VIP colleague in the situation, having clear boundaries or contracting (establishing the rules) at the start of meetings. We cannot go around changing other people – we are the ones who have to change our approach or attitude to best manage ourselves.
- Identify the very lovely people you are surrounded with; there is much to be grateful for here. Appreciate them, thank them and acknowledge them. Most of the people you work with will be here. They are wonderful people to have around – make sure they know that.
- Once you have looked at all of the questions above, where is the tipping point for you? How many people do you need in each area for you to retain and maintain your energy levels and passion? We are all different and all have different thresholds – what are yours?

Box clever pledge: Energy

My current box is _____ (Date: _____)

I want to be able to be _____ by _____ (date)

I am going to do the following:

1) _____

2) _____

Annotate the quadrant with your own notes. What have you taken away from this chapter?

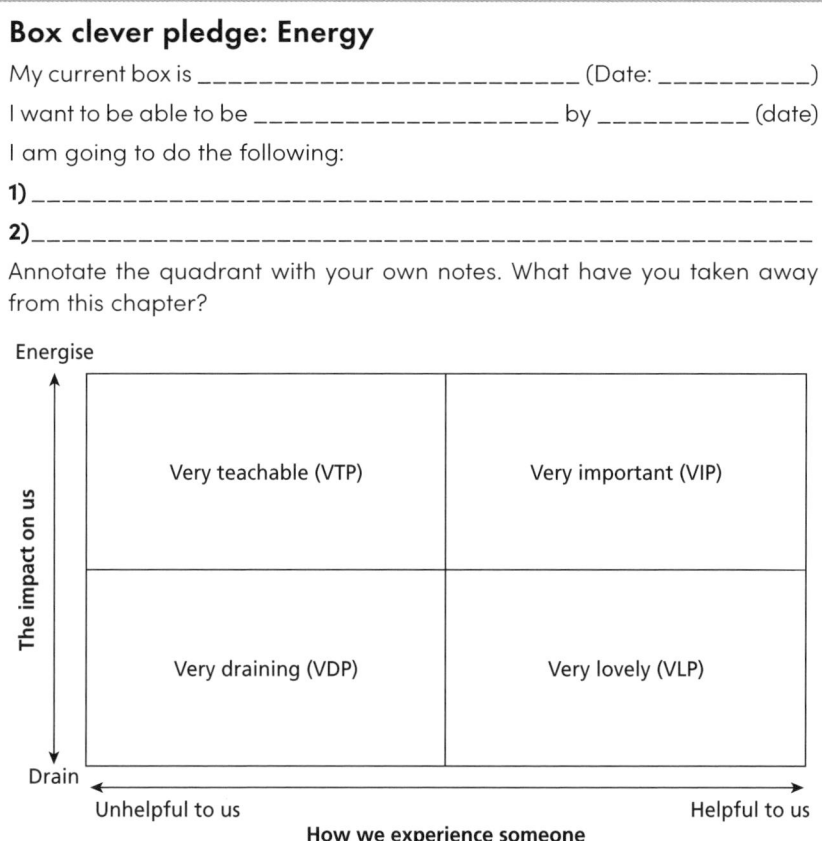

You will find another copy of this quadrant on page 116. Why not put a reminder in your calendar and come back to it in a few months' time and see what has changed?

CHAPTER 11
THE ONE ABOUT WHAT WE SPEND OUR TIME ON

We have explored 10 quadrants in this book so far. These are the 10 that made the final list out of more than 60 that I have been gathering for the last five years – I did warn you that I was fanatical about quadrants! I have deliberately stayed away from ones I used in *Time to Think* 1 and 2 – do head over there if you wish to explore the 'OK Corral' and 'Radical candour' quadrants. I have also tried to avoid the ones that most people will know or have seen. However, there is one of these 'popular quadrants' that I feel I must include in this book: the Eisenhower Matrix.

You will find the Eisenhower Matrix everywhere; it is known by different names and there are different versions, but the premise is the same. Below is my slightly adapted version. This quadrant is a tool for deciding action; it seems fitting, at the end of our time together, to focus on this one last.

Dwight D. Eisenhower was the 34th President of the United States and served two terms between 1953 and 1961. Before he became president, he was a distinguished general in the US Army with a long and impressive track record of innovation and success. He was incredibly productive but still invested time in his hobbies of golfing and oil painting, not seeing it as a case of work or play but making time to do both. This was possible because of the way he was able to sustain his productivity over many decades, and the Eisenhower Matrix is how he made it all happen. Eisenhower knew the difference between 'urgent' and 'important', saying, 'What is important is seldom urgent and what is urgent is seldom important.'

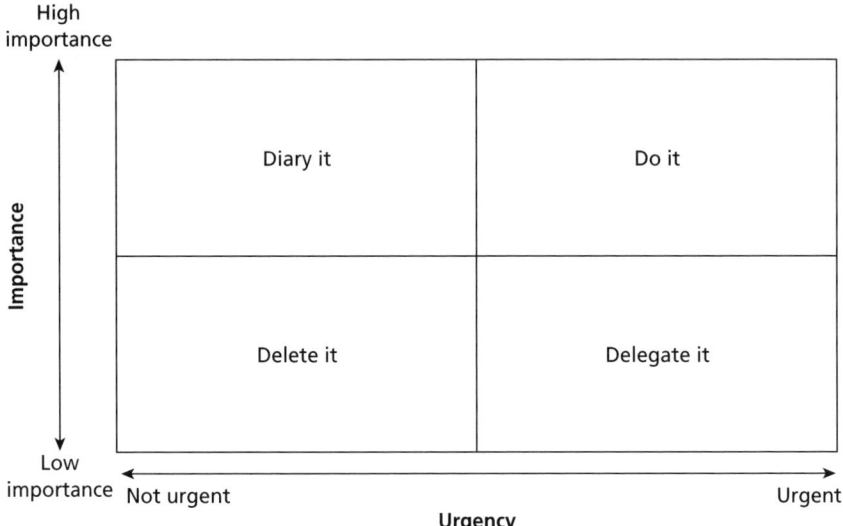

Unpacking the boxes

In his book, *Atomic Habits*, James Clear argues that when we struggle to know what is urgent and what isn't, we can ask ourselves two questions:

1. What am I working toward?
2. What are the core values that drive my life?

These questions help focus our thinking. If we are not clear what we are trying to achieve, then the temptation is to give equal importance to everything that comes our way.

Do it

It needs to happen now. Do not delay, start acting even if you start small – START! The temptation is to put most things in this box and then burn the candle at both ends trying to achieve it – that is not what this box is for. If this is your temptation, start with what to delete first. If we all attempted to do less, we would be more productive, but we struggle with the idea of eliminating anything from the list.

The risk in this box is that we are driven by what is at the top of our inbox and essentially a turn of events (or our teams) dictates where our time goes. Although we need to get the 'urgent' done, not everything is urgent – even if people make it sound like it is! If something is a clarion call, then we move; we have to be all in. But if it's not of crucial importance, we may choose not to act.

Some leaders who use this method attempt to keep this box empty. They argue that if we are managing the other three boxes well, very little would need to be in this urgent and important box. Although this is a challenging task, if we start getting overwhelmed by what is in this box, something has gone wrong somewhere else.

Diary it

It can wait, but it still has to be done, so find a free slot in the diary and book it out to focus on the issue. These ones can be a little seductive in that we may be kicking the can down the road and not tackling the issue. If something is important but not urgent, it needs to be done at some point. Putting it in the diary is the way to keep it in focus without getting involved at the expense of more urgent things.

Typically, in this box you may have things like long term strategy, getting fit and healthy, re-thinking strategy or other big issues to resolve. This is what Dan Heath calls 'upstream thinking', where we are not in the urgent (and the panic!) of the 'downstream' but we are able to think further ahead and plan what needs to happen. This box is altogether calmer than the 'do it' box. The risk is that because it looks calmer, we ignore the issue and head back into the chaos of the top right.

In *Upstream*, Dan Heath writes:

> *Saving the day feels awfully good and heroism is addictive. We all have colleagues who actually seem to relish those manic, 'stay up all night to meet the critical deadline' adventures. And it's not that the day doesn't need saving, sometimes, but we should be wary of this cycle of behaviour. The need for heroism is usually evidence of systems failure.*

If we are caught in everything being urgent all the time, perhaps we may have systems failure somewhere else. The items in the 'diary it' box often deal with the reasons for systems failure. We mustn't let our love of the 'downstream rescue' distract us from tackling the things that really matter.

Delete it

This is neither urgent nor important, and although it may be interesting it isn't the priority right now. Delete it. Perhaps re-visit it at another time. We struggle with deleting anything, so admitting to yourself that a task that goes in here is a waste of time can feel like a big step. Sometimes, the things we spend our time on are not on the list at all but take all our time, whether it be scrolling through social media or clearing the inbox. We can lose hours to these activities when other things are being neglected. Sometimes we have to delete the distractions around us so we can focus on the task at hand.

Delegate it

It is urgent but not for you to do. It may be that the content of this box isn't for you to act on at all, but for your colleagues to work through. Ensure you explain the delegated tasks well so people know what your 'done' looks like.

Stepping out of the box

The Eisenhower Matrix is often used for tasks and to work out what is urgent and what is important. However, it can also be used for our own change or change within our teams. Try using it to plot out your leadership focus, or who you want to *be*, not just what you have to *do*.

- As you look back over your notes and pledges from each chapter, what are the issues that you need to address now? Is it the conflict in your team, or your own blind spots?
- Who do you want to be as a leader? Are these values reflected in the way you spend your time?
- What are the issues you need to discuss with your team? What is holding them back from being even better and when are you going to take the time to explore this?
- What are you deleting that needs to remain? Are we cancelling one-to-one meetings that would really be helpful for us and our organisation? Should they not be deleted, but instead be scheduled sensibly?
- Look at your diary – when is time going to be scheduled to give these issues time and consideration? It doesn't have to be a whole day – sometimes it can be as little as 15 minutes. If you want to move something forward, you need to give it your time and attention. It may not even be time to 'do' anything – it may be giving yourself time to stop and think. Removing a meeting (because it could be an email, for example) so you have time to think is important. We cannot make good decisions if we are not stopping to reflect.
- Do you want to live constantly in the downstream? If the answer is no, and you want to get upstream more often, you have to plan for it.

CHAPTER 11 THE ONE ABOUT WHAT WE SPEND OUR TIME ON

Box clever pledge: Our time

My current box is _____ (Date: _____)

I want to be able to be _____ by _____ (date)

I am going to do the following:

1) _____

2) _____

Annotate the quadrant with your own notes. What have you taken away from this chapter?

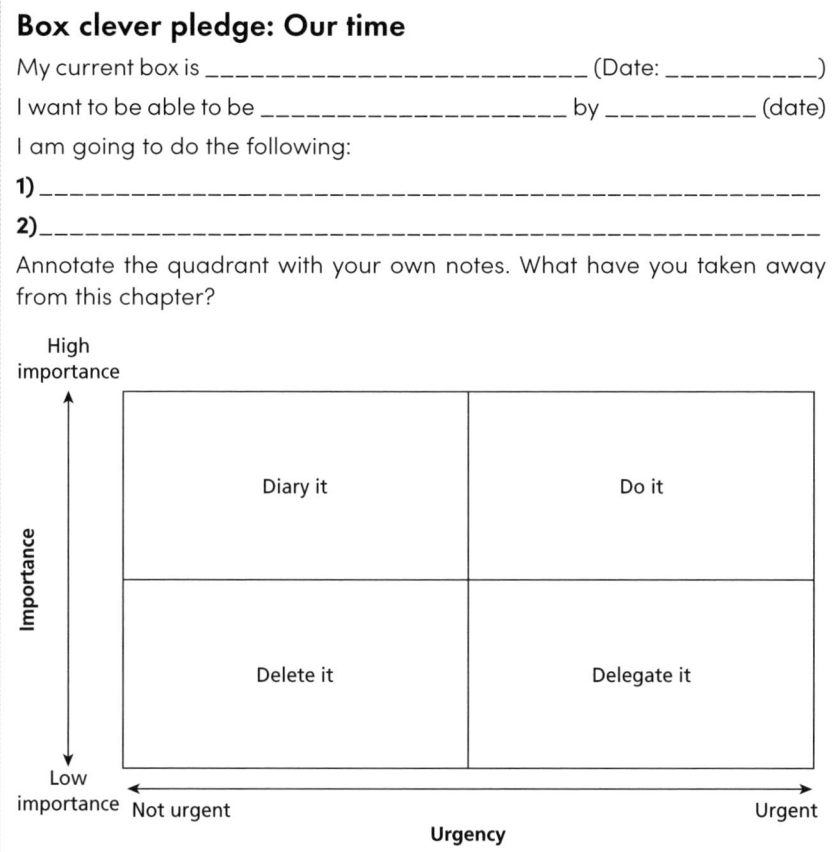

You will find another copy of this quadrant on page 117. Why not put a reminder in your calendar and come back to it in a few months' time and see what has changed?

FINAL THOUGHTS

You have just experienced the 11 greatest hits of my quadrant collection! They have covered a whole range of topics, and some of them will have been provocative, challenging or perhaps comforting because now you have found a name for some things you have been seeing and experiencing. They are tools that can identify where you may be now and where you want to go next and how you are going to make that move. If you have been annotating as you have been going, you may well have lots of notes to work through. I hope you give yourself the time to continue to think about whatever it is you have identified.

I want to end our time together by reflecting on some other boxes – the building blocks that I have found so helpful in my own life and leadership and you may recognise in yours too. These building blocks are what make our own change possible and can inspire others to change. They are things that help me keep my own perspective and, I hope, get the best out of the people I work with. Your building blocks may be different (and that is great!) but spend some time exploring what they are.

My top 10 building blocks

1. Control the chatter in your own mind; 'arrest' negative thoughts that come wandering through your head uninvited and interrogate them. They may have broken in, but that doesn't mean we can't 'arrest' and remove. Notice what that chatter is doing and talk positively to yourself. Be kind to yourself, even when you make mistakes!
2. Pay attention to where your attention is going. What is living in your head rent free? What is taking all of your time and thought? Is that edifying to you and others?
3. Know that you are braver than you think. Look back on where you have been; you have done hard things before and you can do them again.
4. Give people the benefit of the most positive interpretation. Remember that humans are usually trying to do the best they can and are struggling with unseen things, just like you are. Instead of assuming that people

are out to get you (or they have deliberately been this or that), assume something less dramatic and more gracious.

5. Actually care about people – don't just pretend to care. Actions speak louder than words here. If we say we care, we need to know people feel cared for and make a deliberate effort to tell people we value them and are grateful for them.

6. Don't ask others to do what you're not prepared to do yourself. That doesn't mean you have to do it yourself, but it is a helpful way of checking whether what you are asking is not as reasonable as you may think!

7. Don't be afraid to tell people you need them, because you do. The only way you can be a leader is if others are following. We need people. We don't want to come across as needy or intense, but the reality is that we need people around us who we trust and who energise us. Asking for help or asking people for what you need doesn't make you weak – it makes you a human. It's healthy and we should ask; the research suggests that connection happens when people are asked if they can help – they like it! Leadership is a team sport; so is change.

8. Be slow to judge and quick to listen. Notice that you have had a reaction but then really listen to people and find out more. Don't let your own reaction stand in the way of learning that can take place.

9. Find the things that bring you joy – however small – and do them regularly. It's no secret to most people who know me that baths, books, bookshops and coffee shops are my thing and have been since I was 12. These are small things, but they can re-balance me so quickly. They bring me little flickers of joy in everyday life.

10. Face the fear and do it scared if you have to! All of us have wobbles in confidence every now and again. Most of us are not scared of the monster under the bed we used to fear, but we have new monsters. Now we are scared about whether we can turn the organisation around or if we are doing a good enough job. We have to face the fear, investigate whether what we are scared of is 'false evidence appearing real', and then we pick ourselves up and go again. We face the facts, we stare down the situation, we find optimism in the fact we are going to try to make a change… and then we go!

I hope in reading this book, you have found some things that you can take away and use. Perhaps you have found a new language that will help focus your thoughts (and therefore your energy) in the coming weeks. I hope you have also realised that it isn't just you; the struggles, dilemmas or tensions you face are the same challenges many of us experience. Sometimes just knowing that can help make us feel a little safer and a whole lot braver.

Let me leave you with one of my favourite quotations. It's what I want to do, and I hope it's what you want to do too. If so, then perhaps we can do it together:

> *Walk with the dreamers, the believers, the courageous, the cheerful, the planners, the doers, the successful people with their heads in the clouds and their feet on the ground. Let their spirit ignite a fire within you to leave this world a better place than when you found it.*
>
> **Wilfred Peterson**
> **Author of *The Art of the Living***

APPENDIX 1 – RECOMMENDED RESOURCES

Stepping out of the box: A leadership prescription
I often view books, blogs and podcasts like a prescription for the issue that I am struggling with. Since writing both *Time to Think* books, I am often asked to recommend books that will help people with certain common issues. I have taken the most common issues I am asked about and hope that the following list may be of help!

On the usual podcast platforms
The PiXL Pearl podcast – 10 minutes of leadership reflection. A story, how it can be applied to our lives and then some questions to ask ourselves.

The PiXL Leadership Bookclub Podcast – I interview school leaders on non-educational leadership books and see how they have applied their thinking to their context. These are appropriate for people outside of education too. A * next to titles indicates it has been discussed on the podcast.

How can I learn about how I tick?
- *Insight: The Power of Self-awareness in a Self-deluded world* – Tasha Eurich*
- *Triggers: Creating Behavior That Lasts – Becoming the Person You Want to Be* – Marshall Goldsmith
- *Mojo: How to Get It, How to Keep It, How to Get It Back If You Lose It* – Marshall Goldsmith

Do you struggle with vulnerability?
- *Dare to Lead: Brave Work. Tough Conversations. Whole Hearts.* – Brené Brown*
- *Untamed: Stop Pleasing, Start Living* – Glennon Doyle

How can I be a better listener?
- *Time to Think: Listening to Ignite the Human Mind* – Nancy Kline
- *The Promise That Changes Everything: I Won't Interrupt You* – Nancy Kline*

Do you feel fearful?
- *Fear Less: How to Win at Life Without Losing Yourself* – Dr Pippa Grange
- *Ruthlessly Caring: And Other Paradoxical Mindsets Leaders Need to be Future-Fit* – Amy Walters Cohen*
- *Braving the Wilderness: Reese's Book Club: The Quest for True Belonging and the Courage to Stand Alone* – Brené Brown

Have you lost your joy in work and life?
- *Love and Work: How to Find What You Love, Love What You Do, and Do It for the Rest of Your Life* – Marcus Buckingham*
- *Wintering: The Power of Rest and Retreat in Difficult Times* – Katherine May

Do you want to understand more about your emotions?
- *The Four Tendencies: The Indispensable Personality Profiles That Reveal How to Make Your Life Better (and Other People's Lives Better, Too)* – Gretchen Rubin
- *Atlas of the Heart: Mapping Meaningful Connection and the Language of Human Experience* – Brené Brown
- *The Book You Want Everyone You Love To Read (and Maybe a Few You Don't)* – Philippa Perry
- *Bittersweet: How Sorrow and Longing Make Us Whole* – Susan Cain
- *How to be Sad: Everything I've Learned About Getting Happier, by Being Sad, Better* – Helen Russell

Do you want to understand the role of belonging and connection?
- *Belonging: The Ancient Code of Togetherness* – Owen Eastwood
- *The Joy of Work: 30 Ways to Fix Your Work Culture and Fall in Love with Your Job Again* – Bruce Daisley*

How do I get into better habits?
- *Atomic Habits: The Life-changing million-copy* – James Clear
- *Drive: The Surprising Truth About What Motivates Us* – Daniel H. Pink*
- *Change Leader: Learning to Do What Matters Most* – Michael Fullen

How can I feel more hopeful/optimistic?
- *Hope for Cynics: The Surprising Science of Human Goodness* – Jamil Zaki
- *Find Your Way: Unleash Your Power and Highest Potential* – Carly Fiorina
- *Humankind: A Hopeful History* – Rutger Bregman
- *A Beginner's Guide to Dying* – Simon Boas (more hopeful than it sounds!)

How do we create strong cultures in our workplace?
- *Radical Candor: Be a Kick-Ass Boss Without Losing Your Humanity* – Kim Scott *
- *Fierce Conversations: Achieving Success in Work and in Life, One Conversation at a Time* – Susan Scott*
- *The Fearless Organization: Creating Psychological Safety in the Workplace for Learning, Innovation, and Growth* – Amy Edmondson
- *The Culture Code: The Secrets of Highly Successful Groups* – Daniel Coyle*
- *Leadership: Plain and Simple* – Steve Radcliffe
- *Glad We Met: The Art and Science of 1:1 Meetings* – Steven G. Rogelberg*

How can I look again at the issue of my workload?
- *Essentialism: The Disciplined Pursuit of Less* – Greg McKeown*
- *Deep Work: Rules for Focused Success in a Distracted World* – Cal Newport*
- *Happier Hour: How to Spend Your Time for a Better, More Meaningful Life* – Cassie Holmes
- *Four Thousand Weeks: Time and How to Use It* – Oliver Burkeman

How can I overcome people pleasing?
- *Please Yourself: How to Stop People-pleasing and Transform the Way You Live* – Emma Reed Turrell*
- *Jerks at Work: Toxic Coworkers and What to do About Them* – Tessa West*

Anything specifically for women in leadership?
- *How Women Rise: Break the 12 Habits Holding You Back from Your Next Raise, Promotion, or Job* – Sally Helgesen and Marshall Goldsmith*
- *See Jane Lead: 99 Ways for Women to Take Charge at Work* – Lois P. Franke

APPENDIX 2 – COPIES OF ALL THE QUADRANTS

	Known to self	Not known to self
Known to others	Open area	Blind spot
Not known to others	Hidden area	Unknown

Luft, J. and Ingham, H. (1955). 'The Johari Window, a graphic model of interpersonal awareness'. Proceedings of the western training laboratory in group development. Los Angeles: University of California, Los Angeles.

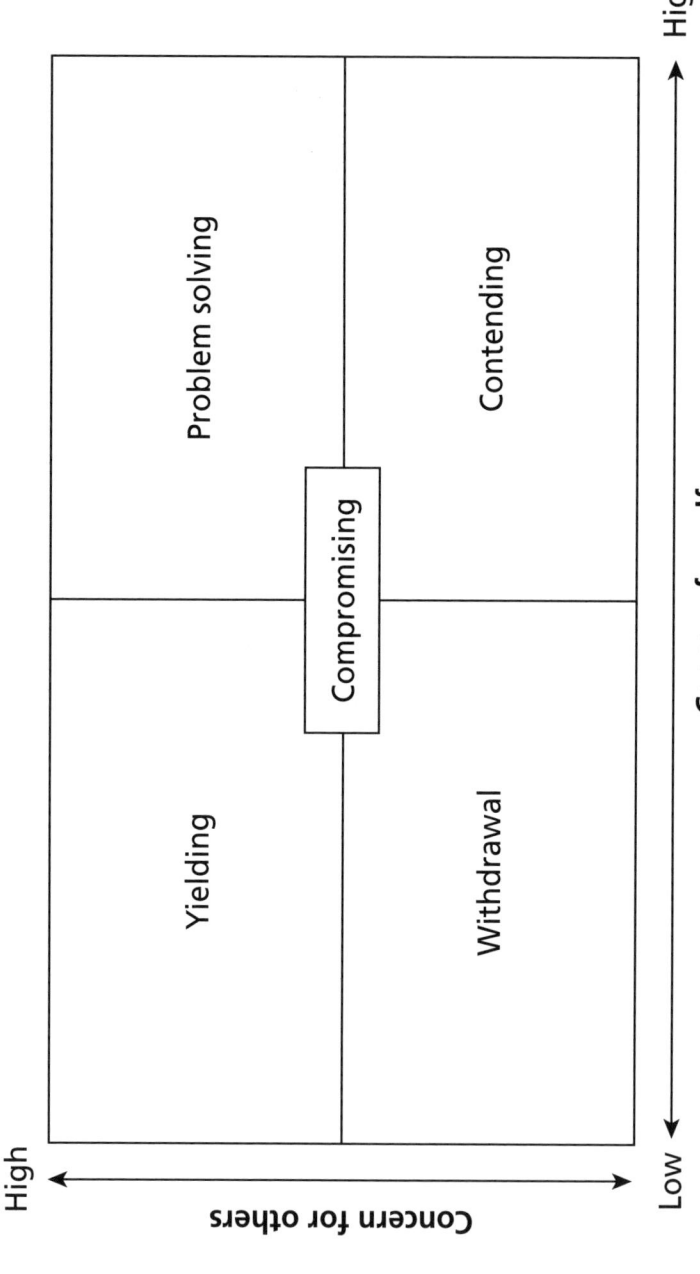

Ramsbotham, Oliver, Woodhouse, Tom and Miall, Hugh (2005). *Contemporary Conflict Resolution: The Prevention, the Management and Transformation of Deadly Conflicts*. Cambridge, Polity Press.

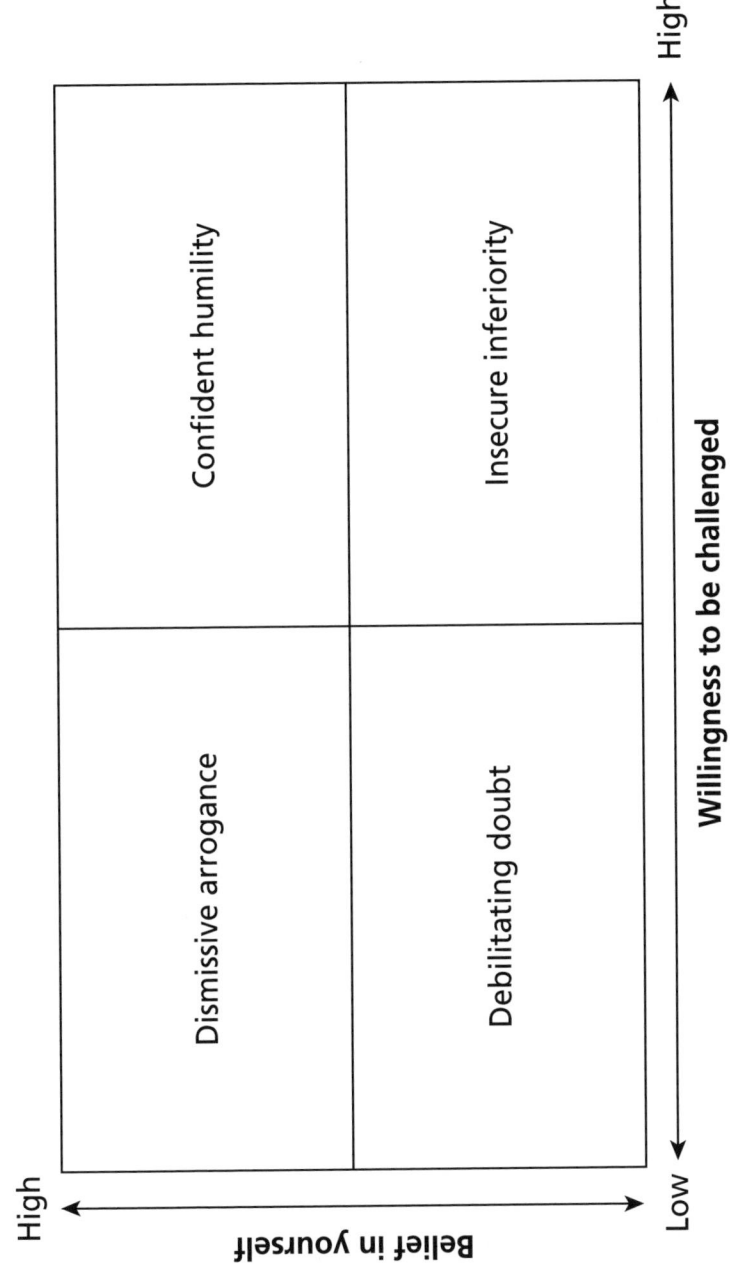

Quadrant devised by Rachel Johnson

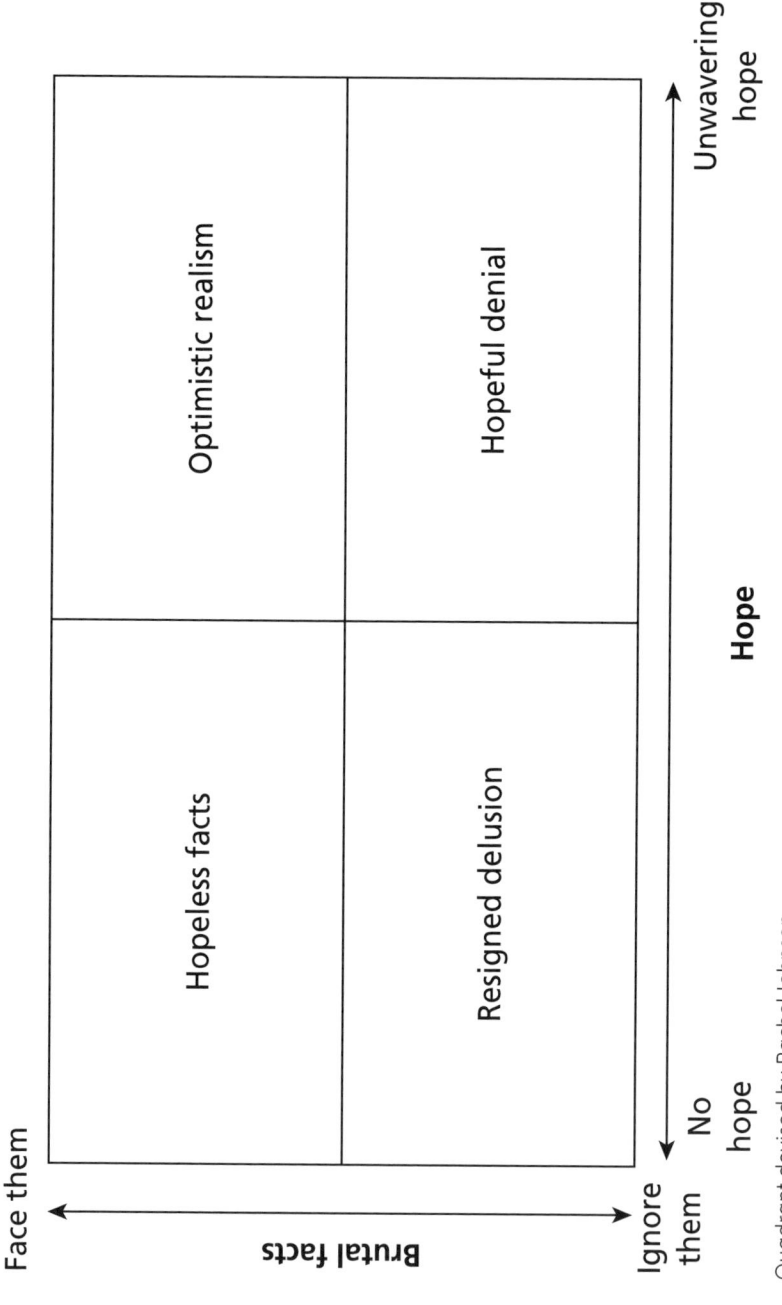

Quadrant devised by Rachel Johnson

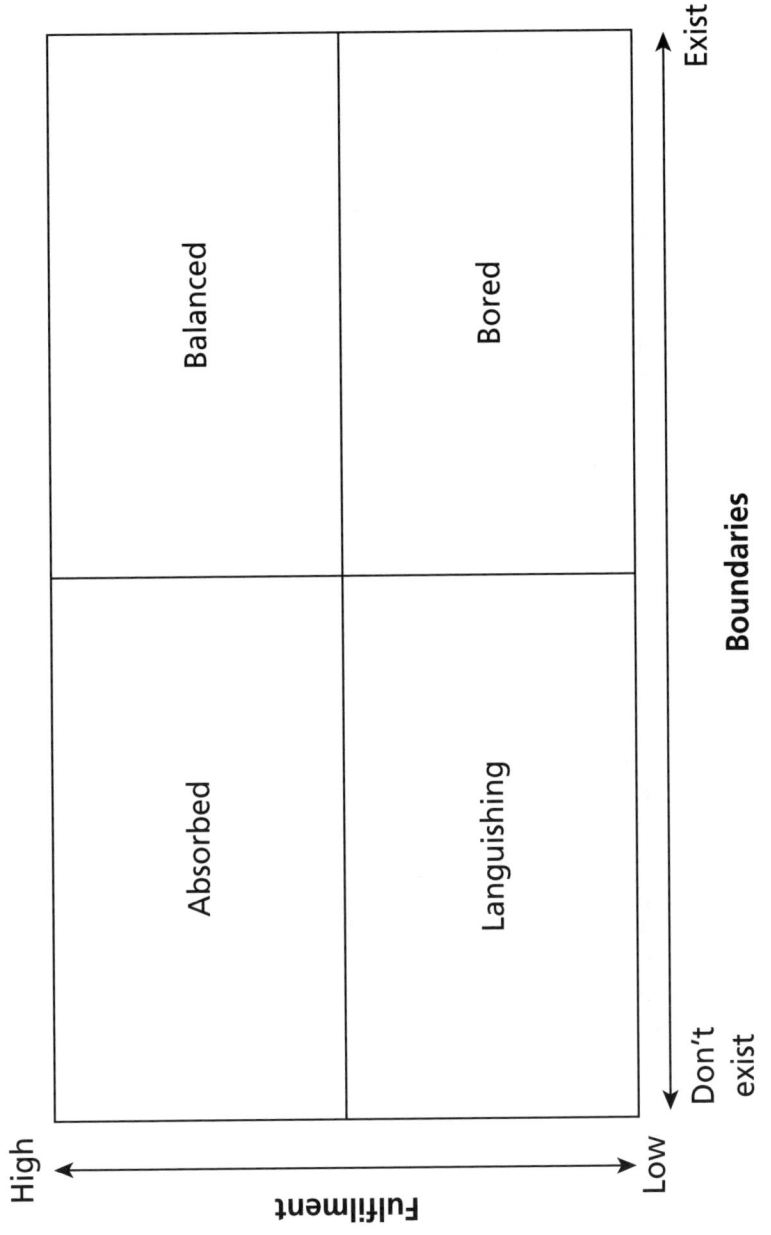

Quadrant devised by Rachel Johnson

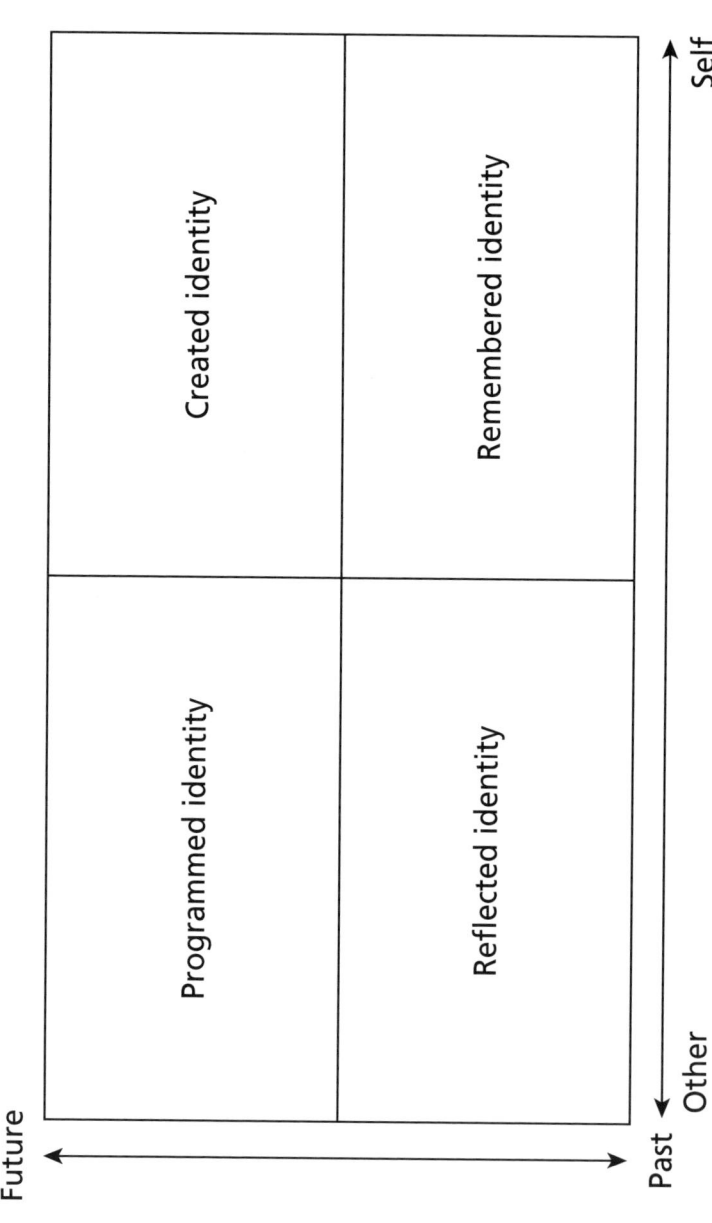

Goldsmith, Marshall with Reiter, Mark (2010). *Mojo: How to Get It, How to Keep It, How to Get It Back When You Lose It.* Profile Books, pp. 44.

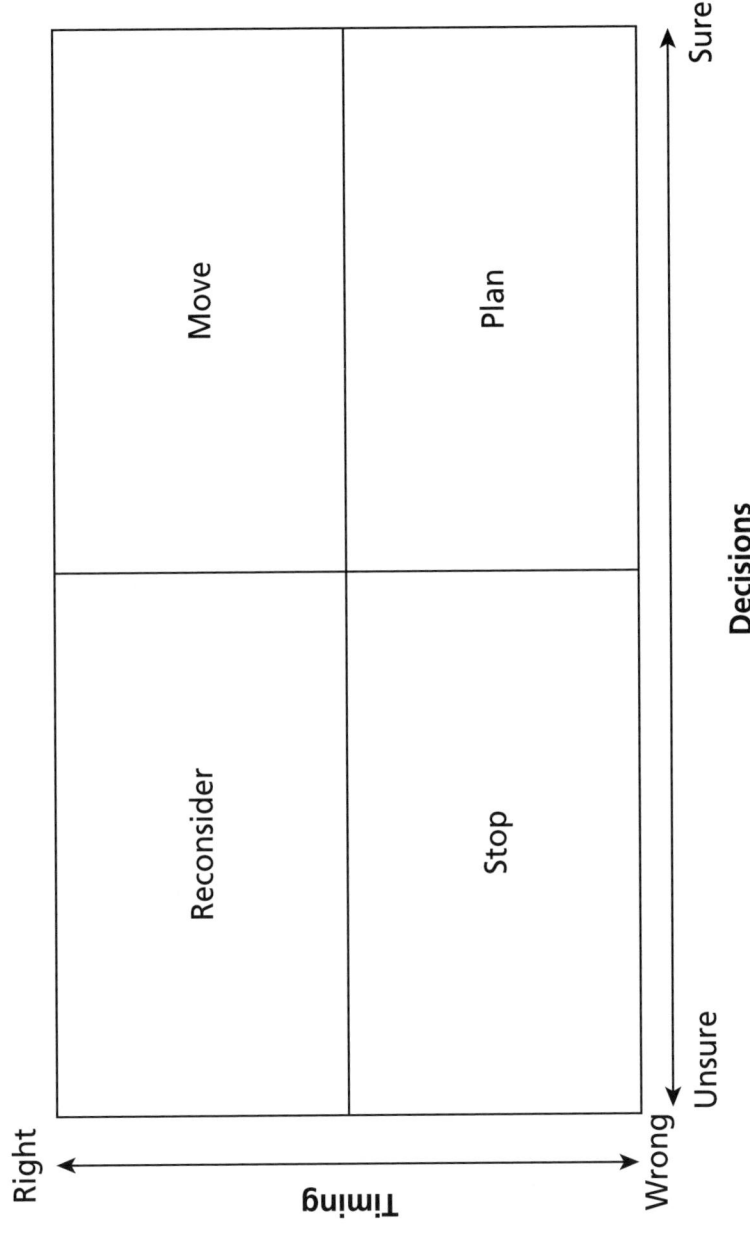

Quadrant devised by Rachel Johnson

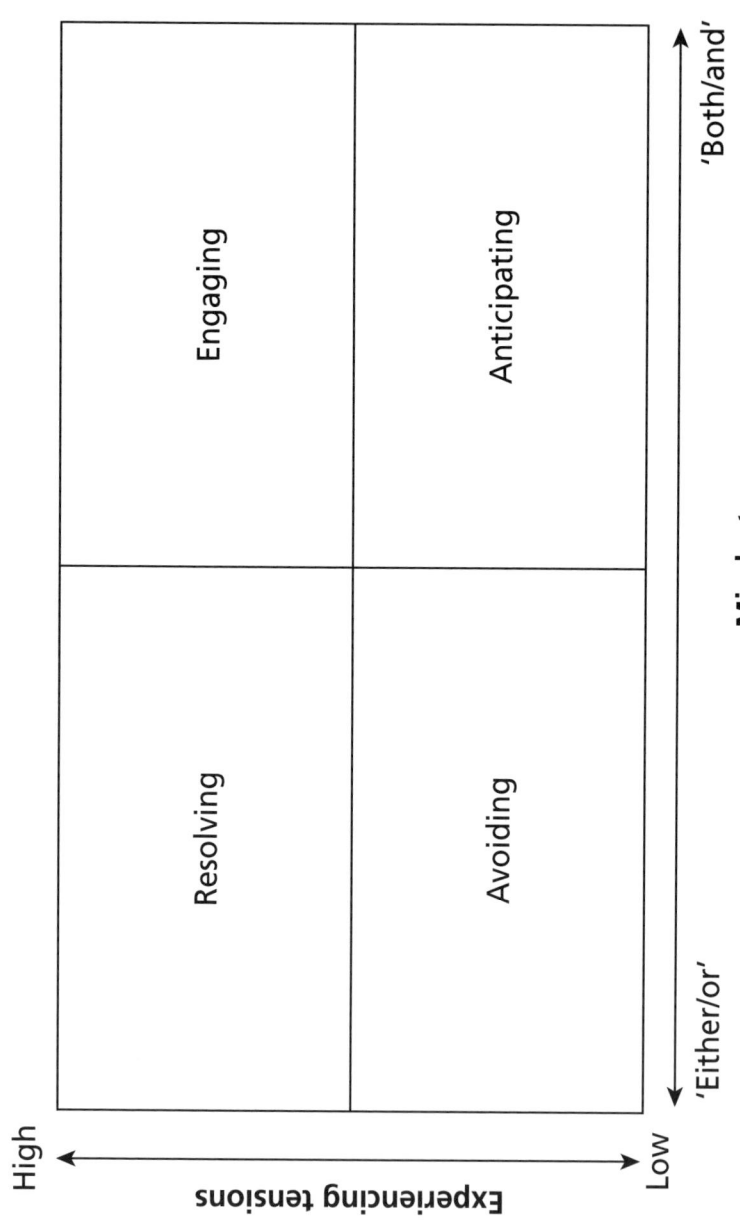

Smith, Wendy K, and Lewis, Marianne W (2022). *Both/And Thinking: Embracing Creative Tensions to Solve Your Toughest Problems.* Harvard Business Press.

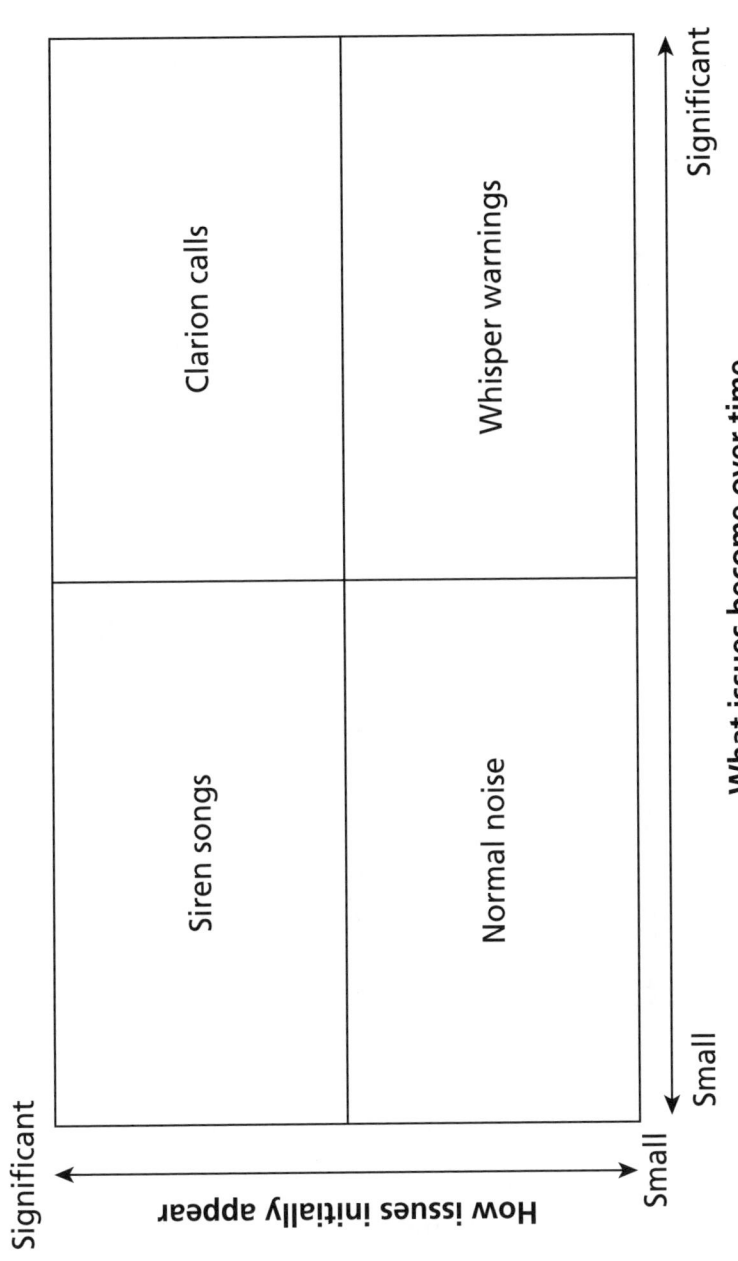

Nohria, Nitin (2024). 'Leaders Must React: A Framework for Responding to Unforeseen events'. Harvard Business Review. Available at: https://hbr.org/2024/01/leaders-must-react (Accessed 18 January 2025).

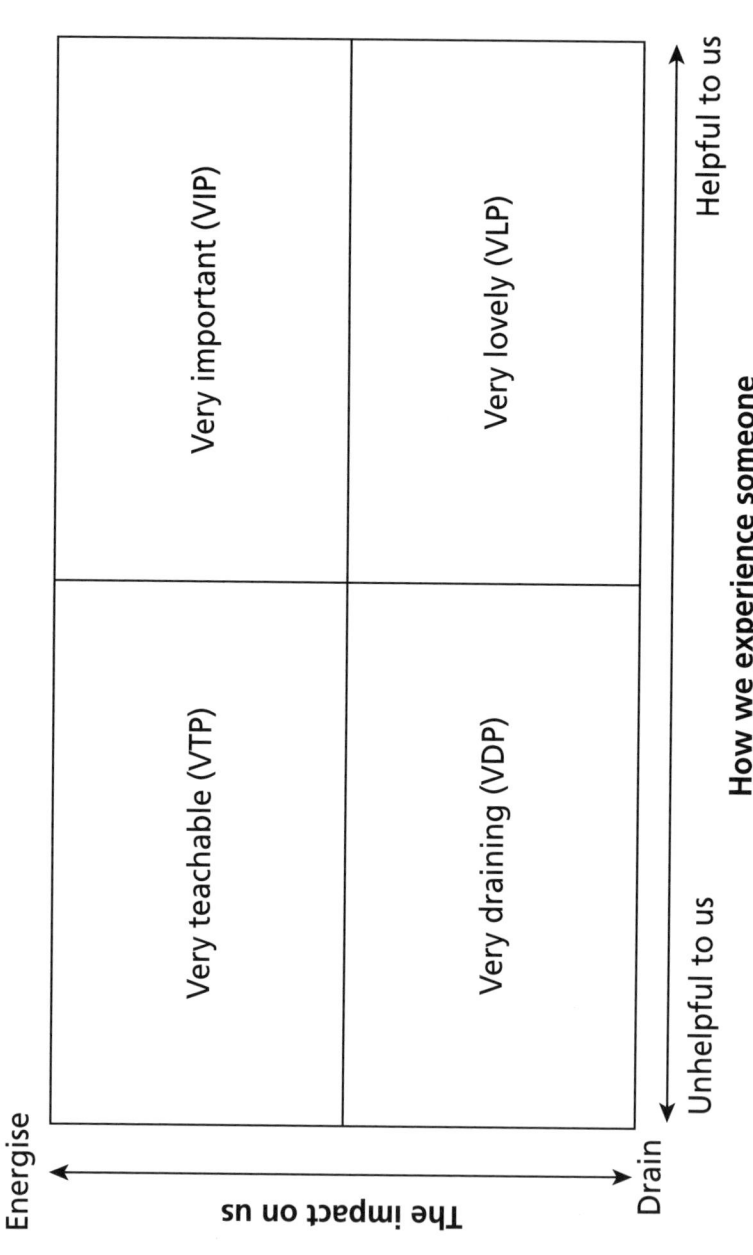

Devised by Rachel Johnson, inspired by McDonald, Gordan (1986). Restoring Your Spiritual Passion. Thomas Nelson Publishers.

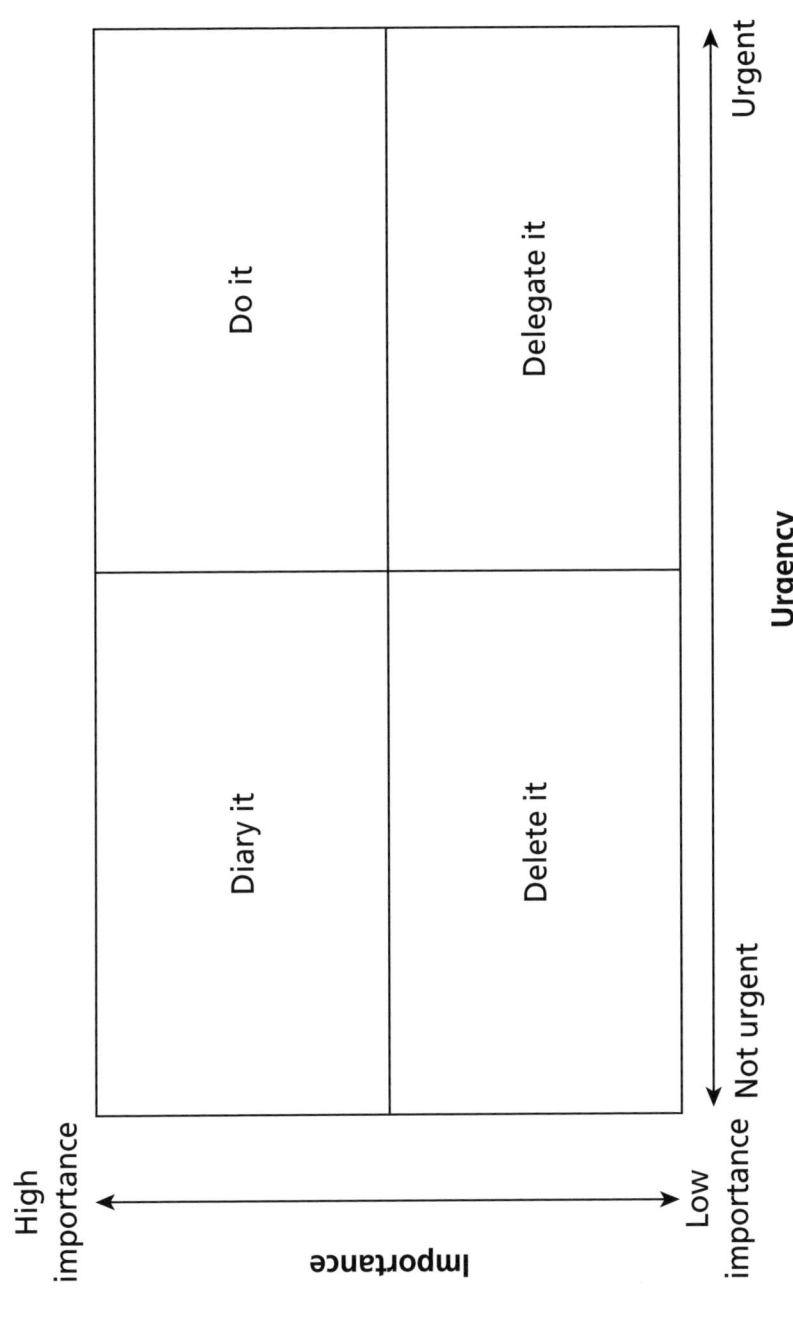

The Eisenhower Matrix (adapted by Rachel Johnson)

BIBLIOGRAPHY

Books

Barber, Michael. (2021) *Accomplishment: How to Achieve Ambitious and Challenging Things*. Penguin, Allen Lane.

Clear, James. (2018) *Atomic Habits: The Life-changing million-copy*. Avery.

Eurich, Dr Tasha. (2013) *Bankable Leadership: Happy People, Bottom-line Results, and the Power to Deliver Both*. Greenleaf Book Group Press.

Edmondson, Amy C and Harvey, Jean-Francois. (2017) *Extreme Teaming: Lessons in Complex, Cross-sector Leadership*. Emerald Publishing.

Goffee, Rob and Jones, Gareth. (2006) *Why Should Anyone Be Led by You?: What It Takes to Be an Authentic Leader*. Harvard Business School Press

Goldsmith, Marshall. (2015) *Triggers: Creating Behavior That Lasts – Becoming the Person You Want to Be*. Profile Books.

Goldsmith, Marshall with Reiter, Mark. (2010) *Mojo: How to Get It, How to Keep It, How to Get It Back If You Lose It*. Profile Books.

Goleman, Daniel and Cherniss, Cary. (2023) *Optimal: How to Sustain Excellence Every Day*. Penguin.

Grant, Adam. (2021) *Think Again: The Power of Knowing What You Don't Know*. Penguin.

Heath, Dan (2024) *Upstream: How to Solve Problems Before They Happen*. Penguin.

Keyes, Corey. (2024) *Languishing: How to Feel Alive Again in a World That Wears Us Down*. Penguin.

Kotter, John P. (2014) *Accelerate: Building Strategic Agility for a Faster-moving World*. Harvard Business Review Press.

McDonald, Gordan. (1986) *Restoring Your Spiritual Passion.* Thomas Nelson Publishers.

Paul-Choudhury, Sumit. (2025) *The Bright Side: Why Optimists Have the Power to Change the World.* Canongate.

Peterson, Wilfred (1969) *The Art of Living in The World Today.* Simon & Schuster.

Ramsbotham, Oliver, Woodhouse, Tom and Miall, Hugh. (2005) *Contemporary Conflict Resolution: The Prevention, the Management and Transformation of Deadly Conflicts.* Cambridge, Polity Press.

Robson, David. (2024) *The Laws of Connection: 13 Social Strategies That Will Transform Your Life.* Canongate.

Scott, Kim. (2021) *Just Work: Get Sh*t Done, Fast & Fair.* St Martin's Press.

Smith, Wendy K and Lewis, Marianne W. (2022) *Both/And Thinking: Embracing Creative Tensions to Solve Your Toughest Problems.* Harvard Business Press.

Widdowson, Lucy and Barbour, Paul J. (2021) *Building Top-performing Teams: A Practical Guide to Team Coaching to Improve Collaboration and Drive Organizational Success.* Kogan Press Limited.

Zaki, Jamil. (2024) *Hope for Cynics: The Surprising Science of Human Goodness.* Little Brown.

Websites and blogs

LSE. *Not a joke: leveraging humour at work increases performance, individual happiness, and psychological safety.* Available at: blogs.lse.ac.uk/businessreview/2021/04/28/not-a-joke-leveraging-humour-at-work-increases-performance-individual-happiness-and-psychological-safety/ (Accessed 29/11/24)

Adam Grant. *Post from 4/5/2018.* Available at: x.com/AdamMGrant/status/992416040159186944 (Accessed 29/11/24)

The Decision Lab. *Johari Window.* Available at: thedecisionlab.com/reference-guide/psychology/johari-window (Accessed 19/12/24)

Fearless Culture. *The Johari Window Exercise.* Available at: fearlessculture.design/blog-posts/the-johari-window (Accessed 19/12/24)

The World of Work Project. *The Johari Window: A Helpful Interpersonal Awareness Tool.* Available at: worldofwork.io/2019/07/the-johari-window/ (Accessed 20/12/24)

Harvard Business Review. *Stop Promoting Incompetent Leaders.* Available at: linkedin.com/pulse/stop-promoting-incompetent-leaders-harvard-business-review (Accessed 3rd January 2025)

Harvard Business Review. *CEOs, Don't Let Fear and Paranoia Sink Your Leadership.* Available at: hbr.org/2020/10/ceos-dont-let-fear-and-paranoia-sink-your-leadership (Accessed 29/11/24)

Sage Journals. *Training for Wisdom: The Distanced-Self-Reflection Diary Method.* Available at: journals.sagepub.com/doi/10.1177/0956797620969170 (Accessed 3/1/25)

Greater Good Magazine. *Intellectual Humility Quiz.* Available at: greatergood.berkeley.edu/quizzes/take_quiz/intellectual_humility (Accessed 3/1/25)

Harvard Business Review. *Good Leaders Know You Can't Fight Reality.* Available at: hbr.org/2021/10/good-leaders-know-you-cant-fight-reality (Accessed 29/11/24)

PsychCentral. *The link between hope and well-being.* Available at: psychcentral.com/health/examples-of-hope#hope-and-health (Accessed 3/1/25)

Science Direct. *The role of hope in subsequent health and well-being for older adults: An outcome-wide longitudinal approach.* Available at: sciencedirect.com/science/article/pii/S259011332030002X?via%3Dihub (Accessed 3/1/25)

Ness Labs. *Hope and optimism are on a spectrum.* Available at: nesslabs.com/hope-optimism (Accessed 1/3/25)

Carnegie Mellon University. *Revised life orientation test.* Available at: cmu.edu/dietrich/psychology/pdf/scales/LOTR_Scale.pdf (Accessed 9.1.25)

Harvard Business Review. *Driving Fulfilment at Work through Real Human-Centered Leadership.* Available at: harvardbusiness.org/wp-content/uploads/2024/03/Driving-Fulfillment-at-Work-through-Real-Huma-Centered-Leadership.pdf (Accessed 27/11/24)

Forbes. *Employees Not Feeling Fulfilled At Work? Seven Ways Leaders Can Help Them.* Available at: forbes.com/councils/yec/2023/06/13/employees-not-feeling-fulfilled-at-work-seven-ways-leaders-can-help-them/ (Accessed 9.1.25)

Harvard Business Review. *What to Do When Your Heart Isn't in Your Work Anymore.* Available at: hbr.org/2017/07/what-to-do-when-your-heart-isnt-in-your-work-anymore (Accessed 9.1.25)

Gallup. *U.S. Employee Engagement Inches Up Slightly After 11-Year Low.* Available at: https://www.gallup.com/workplace/647564/employee-engagementinches-slightly-year-low.aspx# (Accessed 9.1.25)

Harkn. *Key Findings: Gallup's 2024 State of the Global Workplace Report.* Available at: harkn.com/blog/key-findings-from-gallup-s-2024-state-of-the-global-workplace-report/ (Accessed 9.1.25)

Centre for Army Leadership. *Social Identity as an Essential Leadership Tool.* Available at: army.mod.uk/support-and-training/our-schools-and-colleges/centre-for-army-leadership/leadership-resources/leadership-insights/leadership-insight-no45/ (Accessed 1/3/25)

The Rumsfeld Papers. *Known and Unknown: Author's Note.* Available at: papers.rumsfeld.com/about/page/authors-note (Accessed 1/3/25)

Harvard Business Review. *What CEOs are afraid of.* Available at: hbr.org/2015/02/what-ceos-are-afraid-of (Accessed 29/11/24)

Also by Rachel Johnson

Time to Think: The Things That Stop Us and How to Deal with Them

Time to Think 2: The Things That Stop Our Teams and What to Do About Them

ACKNOWLEDGEMENTS

I have loved planning and writing this book over the last few years. I have an enormous collection of quadrants thanks, in part, to so many people sending me good ones they have spotted to add to mine!

I am very fortunate to have some very special people in my life – my VIPs who believe in me, understand me and support me in so many different ways. They energise me, inspire me and challenge me; we disagree well, laugh well and time spent with them is a joy. Many of their names have appeared in both my other books, and I remain so grateful for each and every one of them. A very special mention to my colleagues and friends, Joe Sparks, Jenny Byrne and Christina Moody, without whom I would be a bit lost.

My husband Paul is one of my VIPs, and this book is dedicated to him. In 2008, I had known him only a few weeks (and we had only been going out for two) when I was knocked over by a car, sustaining injuries that could have been life changing but escaping with two broken legs. He sat with me as I was told I may never walk again. What happened after that should be the subject of another book – and may well be, one day! Suffice to say I walked again eventually, and we got married the following year. Since then, we have had our three children, I have been through the grief of losing both my parents in quick succession, and we have been through the usual ups and downs of life (and some that are not usual). Throughout it all, he has been incredible; the most grounding influence, my biggest supporter who has an amazing ability to stay calm even when faced with the most intense challenges – and we have had a few, including a flood in the kitchen right now as I write! I am so grateful for him. He makes so much of what I do possible.

To Charlotte, Daniel and Matthew – you continue to bring me so much joy. I am so proud of the people you are and are becoming. You also make me laugh every single day!

To the Great Park Gang and Ken Matthews – thank you for all your love and support (and cake and laughter) and for praying this book into existence and praying for me as I worked on it!

To the PiXL team – it remains a joy and privilege to lead you. Your embodiment of our culture and your commitment, determination and enthusiasm for what we do is something I find humbling. Thank you for your unwavering support and for being up for the challenges – the exciting and the terrifying!

And to you, reading this book. Thank you for buying it, for engaging with it and for being so invested in developing yourself and your teams. Your spirit (and your response to what I write) ignites a fire in me. Thank you.